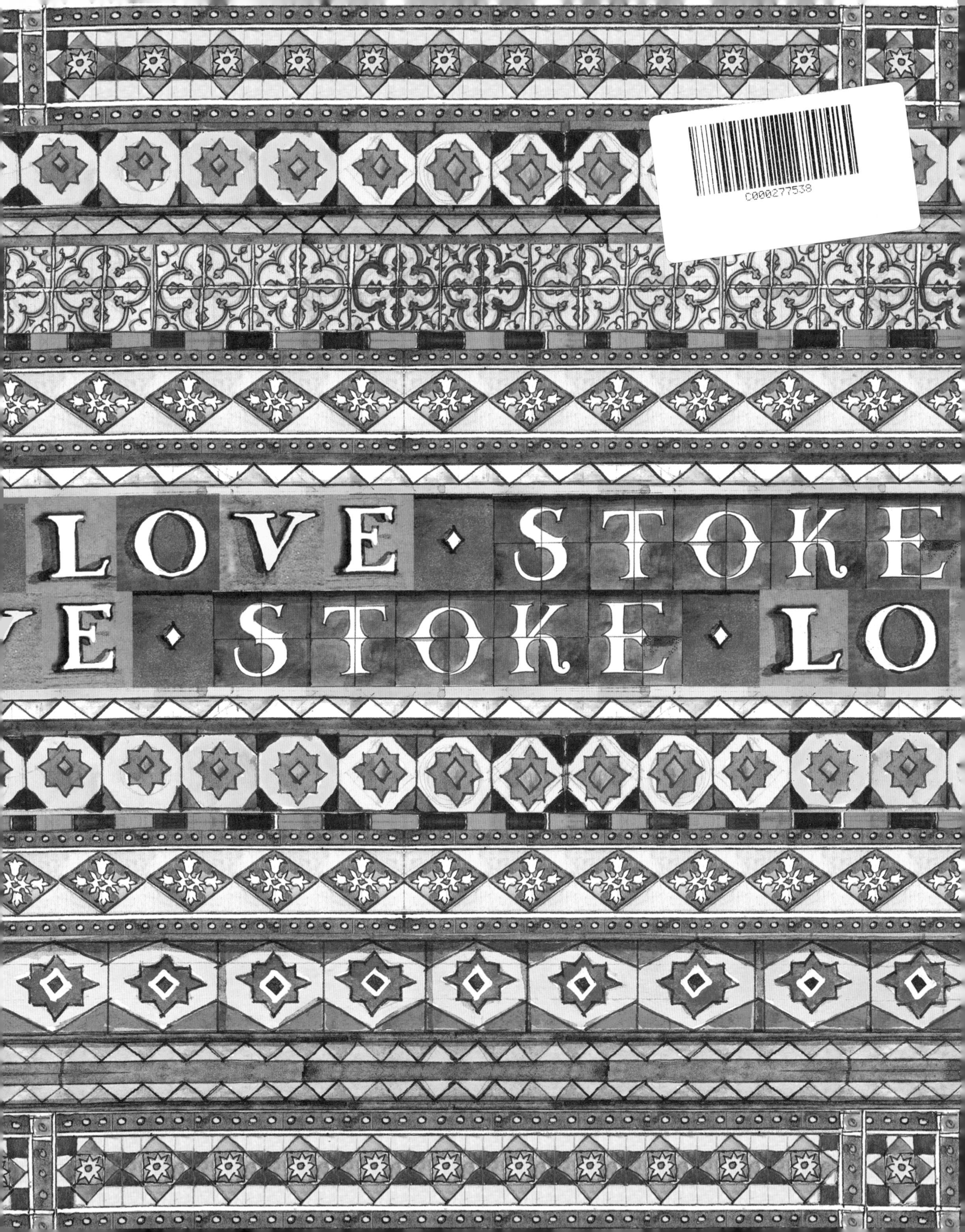
LOVE · STOKE
VE · STOKE · LO

THE LOST CITY OF STOKE-ON-TRENT

THE LOST CITY OF STOKE-ON-TRENT

MATTHEW RICE

F

FRANCES LINCOLN LIMITED
PUBLISHERS

For Margaret

Frances Lincoln Limited
4 Torriano Mews
Torriano Avenue
London NW5 2RZ
www.franceslincoln.com

The Lost City of Stoke-on-Trent

First Frances Lincoln edition 2010

A catalogue record for this book is available from the British Library.

ISBN 978-0-7112-3139-9

Printed and bound in China

9 8 7 6 5 4 3 2 1

CONTENTS

ACKNOWLEDGEMENTS

Stoke-on-Trent has many admirers and a loyal and energetic fan club. Most remarkable are Steve Birks, creator and editor of the potteries.co.uk website, and his regular correspondent David Proudlove. This site is a deep and productive mine of information, down whose shaft I have been regularly returning. They and it are my most important acknowledgement. I have toured Stoke both with my teacher and friend Alastair Langlands and with my patient assistant and friend Will Whittaker. Again Will has also scanned and tidied my often scrappy drawings most brilliantly and uncomplainingly. Boadacea Meath-Baker's splendid and detailed research provided much material and has been invaluable.

More gaps in my knowledge have been filled by Miranda Goodby, ceramics curator of the City Museum, Basil Juda, Sue Evans, Mark Thomas, Jane Caulfield, Hugh Edwards, Hugh Padley, Neil Ewins, Chris Taylor, Tom McCartney, Jacqui Gennane, Geoff Pugh and countless others.

Carolyn Dawnay, my kind agent, and John Nicoll of Frances Lincoln are responsible for this book's existence, and Becky Clarke for its appearance, speedily and tidily put together. While all errors and inaccuracies are all my own work, without the kind but firm editing of Anne Askwith this book would have been formless drivel.

But most of all my thanks and love are due to Emma Bridgewater, whose extraordinary imagination, energy, gritty hard work and devotion to English manufacturing have created jobs for the 200 people who work at our factory in Lichfield Street. That unfashionable and, at times, quixotic achievement has made this book possible, both in causing me to see Stoke from the inside out and in providing the luxury of being able to write about it.

FOREWORD
BY EMMA BRIDGEWATER

When I first stepped off the train at Stoke-on-Trent twenty-five years ago it changed my life.

Before I went there I suppose that, like lots of people, I had studied the Industrial Revolution a little. I knew that Isambard Kingdom Brunel was a good egg, because I loved Paddington station; and I'd heard of Josiah Wedgwood, but was pretty mystified as to the appeal of his nymph-sprigged wares as found in airports all over the world at the time. I had a dim knowledge of the huge transforming changes the revolution had brought to the cities of the Midlands, which sprang up incredibly hastily as people abandoned the countryside to find work in the burgeoning factories producing household goods such as cotton, glass, iron, pottery and much more for our expanding Empire.

Broadly speaking I had always thought of the Industrial Revolution as a thoroughly Good Thing; the railways and canals, coal mines and foundries – well, where would we have been without them? But I had never considered the actual physical facts of all this. I had no idea about its tangible impact, and still less the incredibly long-reaching and doleful aftermath of urban decay and neglect that tagged along at the tail end of our great manufacturing heyday.

During my first (pretty smelly) taxi ride across the city I was fascinated and appalled by the chaos of road works, ring roads, boarded-up shops and run-down terraces. I immediately loved the hundreds of distinctive bottle kilns scattered through this urban sprawl; they were sooty but splendid, solid and friendly, usually with buddlejas growing out of their bulgy sides. The taxi driver was nosy, in a friendly way. Then the kind lady who sold me my first Wright's pie called me 'duck', and I was in. I fell completely for the cheerful griminess of the city and every single decision I made about my business thereafter was made in the shadow of the Potteries.

Growing up in Hertfordshire, and then north Oxford, spending holidays in Norfolk, Northumberland and Cornwall, I had always mourned cottages that looked unloved, and felt drawn to derelict farmhouses and positively tearful about neglected barns and stables. But here in Stoke was uncaring on a really lavish scale: whole terraces of houses tumbling down, chapels beaten into tyre-change workshops and rudely tattooed with graffiti, old factories out of whose broken windows and roofs pigeons flew out in clouds as I passed. While I knew I could never put this right, I dreamed of trying. I developed unstoppable visions of re-opening derelict factories in order to make my designs; I wanted to make the hooters blare out again; I imagined my name in terracotta, in Minton tiles, in wrought iron, over gatehouses now shrouded in corrugated iron and barbed wire.

The prevailing wisdom was – and is – that there is nothing but heartbreak to be had from manufacturing in this country. I was frequently and urgently advised, then and ever since, to get someone else to see to the making (preferably cheaply, abroad) and simply concentrate on the design and marketing of my pottery. I did find someone else to do the making for a while (I had no choice), but I knew that I was committed to Stoke.

So why was I on that train in the first place? How did it all begin? After university (Eng. Lit. at London) I had a job working for some designers for about eighteen months. They were generous employers who refrained from telling me to shut up when I asked endless questions about all aspects of their successful business. In the course of my eighteen months with them I did just about every task available, from sewing on buttons and labels, to selling from the sample collection in New York, to recruiting hundreds of home-knitters to make up orders. I had also done overdraft penance in my father's dynamic publishing business in Cambridge between university terms (until I discovered that waitressing in Covent Garden was more lucrative).

So I really felt fully equipped to start a business. I was not sure what that business would do or sell, until one day, while I was looking for a present for my mother for her birthday, the penny just dropped. I stood in a china shop, feeling cross and frustrated. Surely it should be easy to find a pretty cup and saucer? Why was everything on display so completely irrelevant to her tastes? Kerching. I should make the cup and saucer myself.

Here was the business idea I had been seeking. And after this events moved at speed. I sketched the shapes I envisaged, collecting lots of favourite pieces around me before I started. Then I experimented, helped by a photographer who collected colourful spongeware pottery, and evolved a simple way to handprint a design on to my shapes. The photographer advised setting up a craft pottery in London; but, fresh from battling with home-workers to meet fashion deadlines, I was sure I wanted to produce my designs in 'a factory'. I really did not know what I meant by this; I simply hoped to find a way to get things made on time, preferably in quantities, which did not involve home-workers, as I had had my fill of the stresses that involved. I recognized that I had a sense of inadequacy when faced with the world of craft pottery: I had chosen university over art school, and never felt able to see my ideas for pottery as art. I instinctively veered towards the idea of industrial pottery, and set out to find a way into that world with a dawning sense of connection to it even before my first visit to Stoke-on-Trent.

A graphic designer told me about some recent adventures in pottery – designing beer-pump pulls, jugs and ashtrays as part of a re-branding job for a brewery – in a workshop at Longbridge Hayes in Stoke-on-Trent. He told me to get in touch with a ceramic model maker, who would translate my sketches into models from which to make moulds to cast my shapes in earthenware. He gave me the telephone number and encouraged me to get down to it, saying, 'Come back and tell me how you get on.' So I made an appointment, and then caught the train at Euston and set out to Stoke.

To cut an eventful story short, this same workshop, with the atmospheric address of Chemical Lane, first modelled my shapes and then made batches of undecorated ware for me to sample. In due course, when I started to generate wholesale orders they took over production. I taught the two decorators how to do my patterns and had my colours matched and mixed up for them. So, equipped with sponge printing blocks, which I cut out for them, they could interpret the designs with some freedom, while I retained enough control to ensure that the production was true to my samples.

My first trade fair was in London in April 1985, so I count this as the real start of the company. It was at this same trade fair in the old Derry and Toms building in Kensington High Street that I was to meet Matthew a few years later. From this time on, the core of my business was a trade with a selection of creative shops all over the UK. The pottery was made in batches in Chemical Lane. When it was ready, I would hire a van in London, drive to Stoke, count and pack the orders for each shop into the van, and then deliver them around the country, sleeping on friends' sofas and floors and hurrying to get the van back as soon as I could. Then I would rush out the invoices and, as they fell due, ring customers if they did not pay instantly, so as to have the money in the bank when the invoices from Chemical Lane came through. And so I had started a business, depending on a factory (of sorts) in Stoke-on-Trent. I had no business plan and no capital, but I was under way.

From then on, I spent a great deal of time in Stoke. I stayed in damp farmhouse B&Bs, morosely wallowing in Arnold Bennett's evocative novels and short stories, half loving and half hating the extremely singular qualities of Staffordshire. I subsisted on meat and potato pies in the day time and dire pub food in the evenings, always feeling a bit dehydrated by the ubiquitous clay and plaster dust and as if I might be in the early stages of scurvy – to the extent that I associate a feeling of physical discomfort with my work in the Potteries. (We now have a café alongside the shops in the courtyard of our factory, so the standards of subsistence have improved a bit. At the very least I can now get a decent cup of coffee.) Over the next few years I worked in several different factories; I sought out colour and glaze suppliers, and makers of cardboard boxes, backstamps and brushes; I made friends with model-makers and mould suppliers in grimy backstreet workshops.

Long before starting to design and make pottery I had loved the Victoria and Albert Museum in South Kensington. As a rather solitary student I had spent darkening, rainy afternoons alone on the top floor of the museum, lost in creamware, slip-trailing, blue and white printed wares, lustre and pearlware on a thousand shapes. Once in Stoke I soon found the City Museum and its unbelievably wonderful collection of Staffordshire wares. Suddenly it all started to fall into place as I pored over the shelves and cabinets of bewitching wares. Stoke was where pretty much all the china we ever needed had been made – in these streets, by the forebears of the people I queued up with for the cinema in the evening. Mentally I set aside all the grand and stately china I'd ever looked at, all the one-offs and the show-offs. What I wanted was to focus on the real everyday wares from ordinary homes. I wanted to be a part of the industry and tradition that had created 200 years' worth of Britain's tablewares. The names that recurred in my notes and sketches amount to a roll call of the dead factories of the city: Gray's Pottery, Royal Winton, Midwinter, J. and G. Meakin, Woods, Masons, Foley, Ridgway, Adams and so on, but the huge quantity of humble and unnamed wares are even more indicative of the

city's history of mass, unselfconscious production for a booming market. There is one constant in the shifting scene in Stoke, and that is the towering spirit of ingenuity and creativity which imbues the city and which I always feel hovering in the air there.

All the time I felt a mixture of exhilaration, exhaustion and confusion. How had Stoke evolved into such a different city from Newcastle-upon-Tyne? Or Norwich? Or Bodmin? Why did it feel so cut off from the England I knew? In every shop and factory it seemed that people listened only to the local station, Signal, and read just the one paper, local again, The Sentinel. The Guardian and Radio 4 did not seem to penetrate. Each time I turned off the M6 or jumped into a taxi at the station I approached work there with a mix of glee and dread and a slight suspicion that I had been transported to a different planet. There was always a steep uphill struggle as I wrestled with the outcomes so painfully negotiated last time – firing times, colour matches, quantities, dates, prices, all liable to swift unwelcome changes and compromises. I had plunged into business with breathtaking ignorance. My one advantage was determination and it often seemed as if this was not enough. I was certainly utterly unprepared for the sheer difference of the business from anything I had ever known previously.

So each arrival at Stoke-on-Trent has been full of mixed emotions, and it has been the chief setting for many of the thrills and plenty of the tedium of the last twenty-five years for me. And so too has it been for Matthew: after he and I married, and he joined the company, his professional design background and matching enthusiasm for the tradition of British ceramic design proved invaluable. While I continued to produce almost all of the shape designs, he expanded our patterns no end.

Through countless meetings I've looked out into litter-strewn streets or ruined terraces and grassed-over spoil heaps, perhaps sometimes only half aware of the city as a place that continued to exist when I wasn't there. One of the ways that the life of the place in between trips manifested itself was in the fact that huge gaps would appear from one week to the next as another Victorian factory fell foul of the bulldozer. Over twenty-five years the demolition and change has been perverse and perplexing. The road systems have never not been in a state of utter confusion,

ALTHOUGH LATE ⑲ this factory STILL FOLLOWS the ⑱ CLASSICAL MODEL

and all the while whole communities consisting of schools, pubs, churches, chapels and parks as well as factories have been flattened, as if they were never there. In a final gesture just about all the friendly bottle kilns have been pulled down as well. The awful wastefulness of this must, of course, be set against the benefits of a clean-up that has eradicated much sootiness, and I am quite sure that through neglect much of the old housing stock had deteriorated to a sorry condition. Now where pit spoil heaps, mines and foundries as well as factories once stood there are industrial estates and retail parks full of big sheds offering some new jobs. Some of this must be useful, but the ugliness is a persistent nagging whine.

When I could find the time, ever since my very first visit I always wanted to explore, on foot and by car around the city. More recently this has often been in Matthew's company, which is altogether jollier, as he is endlessly cheered and excited by the architecture of the area. That is, when he is not jumping up and down in fury and indignation about yet more demolition and soulless new development. I share his ideas about preserving as much as possible of what is left. We sometimes picnic in the dramatic hills outside the city among sheep and curlews, and from a distance the contrast between this picturesque moorland landscape and the ugly grey sprawl of the Potteries obviously triggered something in his mind, causing him to resolve to investigate how the city grew, and to address the pressing question of how on earth can anyone bring about some positive changes to the urban landscape.

That is how and why he started on this book. In the process he has delved into the history of the city with characteristic speed, tireless enthusiasm and his own iconoclastic attitude, which uncovers platitude and tears down and turns inside out many received wisdoms about town planning and urban regeneration. All that, and jokes.

EMMA BRIDGEWATER

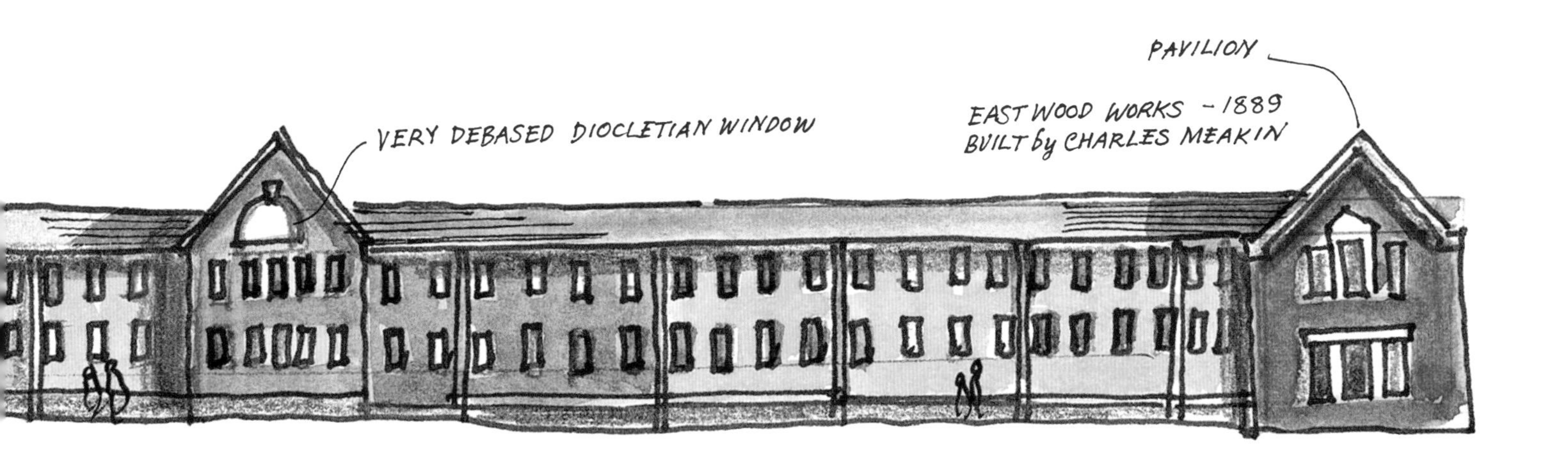

PREFACE

Twenty-five years ago Emma Bridgewater came to Stoke-on-Trent and started a business. You can hear what happened next in the foreword that precedes this.

I am her husband and two years ago I started to take my turn at running the company, which now employs 200 people. So while I had known Stoke a bit for a quarter of a century I began to look more closely. This book is what I found.

Local history books are a mixed bag. Some are reproduced editions of county histories, printed in runs so short that their cost is prohibitive and their print unreadably faint on paper tissue thin. Some are stuffed with compelling black and white photographs of high streets and early ring roads jammed with Ford Anglias, Hillman Imps and Morris Oxfords or with a racy Cortina parked roguishly in front of a long demolished public library. Others still identify a particular field of interest; the author might as well have gathered all three potential readers together one day and passed on his ideas face to face. Some are full of painfully careful research, referenced and noted so that the actual text becomes almost a footnote itself. Yet more pedal half-digested misinformation in a ring of Chinese whispers operated by the profoundly deaf of differing mother tongues. Not only do they fib and muddle but they do so with magisterial authority.

This is not any of these. It is not exhaustive and its facts are selected only to illustrate a ballad of death and destruction with a rather brighter refrain of renewal. It may be your guidebook; there isn't another. It is definitely for my friend Stephen Hyde, whose question 'What book should I read to find out about Stoke and the Potteries?' made me know that I should plough on with this rough outline of what was once one of our great industries and remains a very real bit of manufacturing in a service-dominated economy. But most of all it is a siren calling everyone who cares: lovers of Stoke and of the Staffordshire potteries, councillors, developers, urban renewers and the tens of thousands of visitors who come to this most superficially unlovely of cities each year. Its wail across the brick dust deserts and hoarded wasteground, past the blasted shopping centres and flaking factories, is—

STOP! STOP RIGHT NOW!

Don't knock down another thing. Not another tidy dark-bricked terrace or crumbling manufactory. Not a gate pier, Minton tile or bootscraper of it. Not until we know how to put it right, how to shepherd the last remnants of the Victorian city into some form that recalls and basks in its past as pottery to the world. The grave of Bishop Bell (1883–1958) in Christ Church Cathedral in Oxford states in letters of austere limestone: 'Without forgiveness there can be no regeneration.' Stoke-on-Trent needs to reconcile itself with its past before it can renew.

Pottery has not been benign. With 300 pot banks with their 2,000 bottle kilns smoking into a leaden sky, with a vanished coal and steel industry as well as 200 years of manufacture, poverty and grime, the industry has been poisonous and debilitating, underpaid and often unprofitable for its owners, and has in the last twenty years shrunk by four-fifths. But it does survive. You can see it through windows all over the city, see its factories, walk past them along the Trent and Mersey or Caldon canals, even visit some.

The buildings of a place are the face of its history and this book is about them and their stories. They are all significant, anchors to hold fast to while the place rethinks its character. When that is resolved and Stoke-on-Trent, perfectly situated midway between Manchester and Birmingham and so close to Britain's communication spine, re-emerges it will need all the crumbling façades and church towers, all the bottle kilns and mould sheds, all the pottery owners' houses and the artisan terraces that it can find.

This is a record of some of them today.

MATTHEW RICE
Oxford, March, 2010

MAP OF STOKE

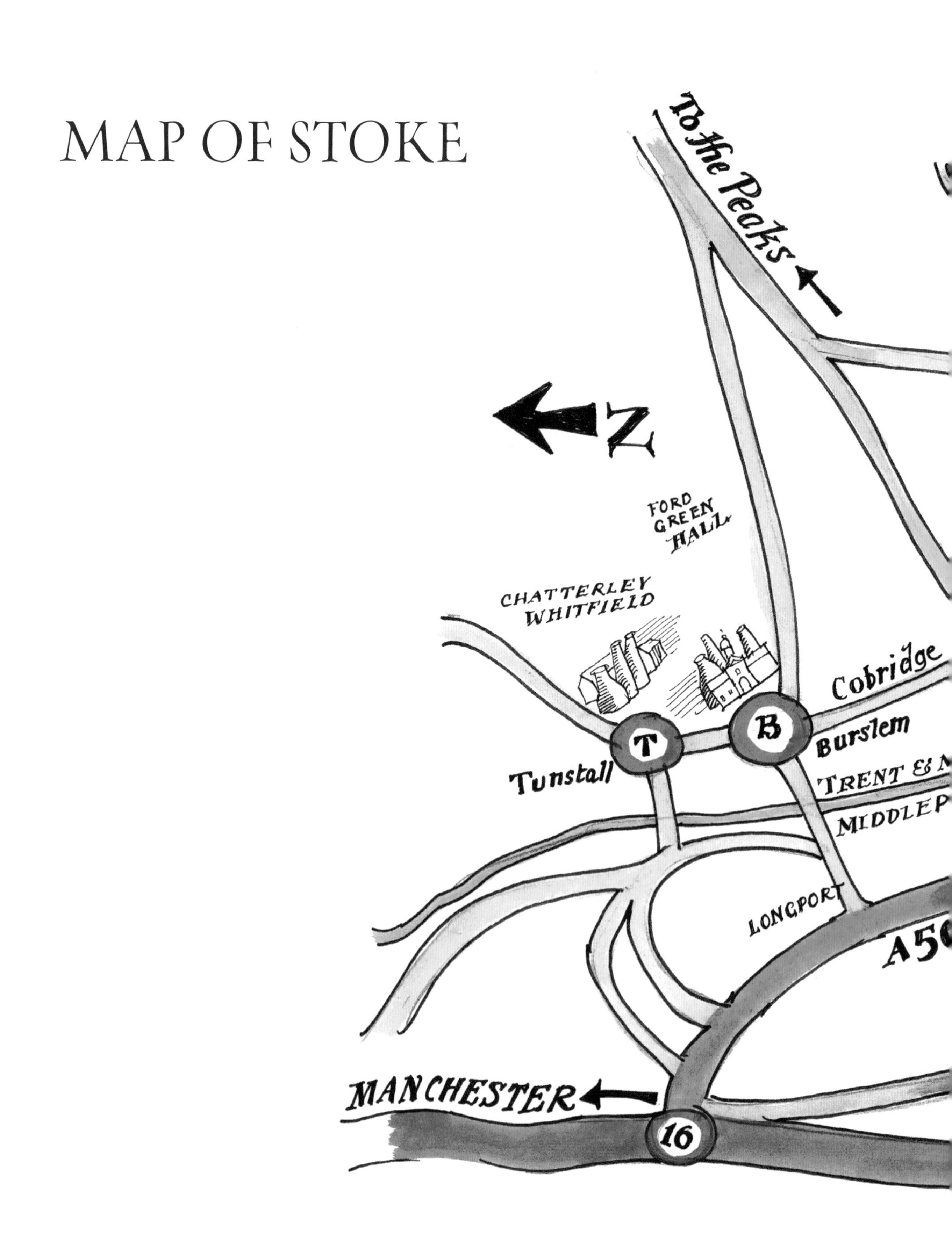
To the Peaks
N
FORD GREEN HALL
CHATTERLEY WHITFIELD
Cobridge
T
B
Burslem
Tunstall
LONGPORT
MANCHESTER
16

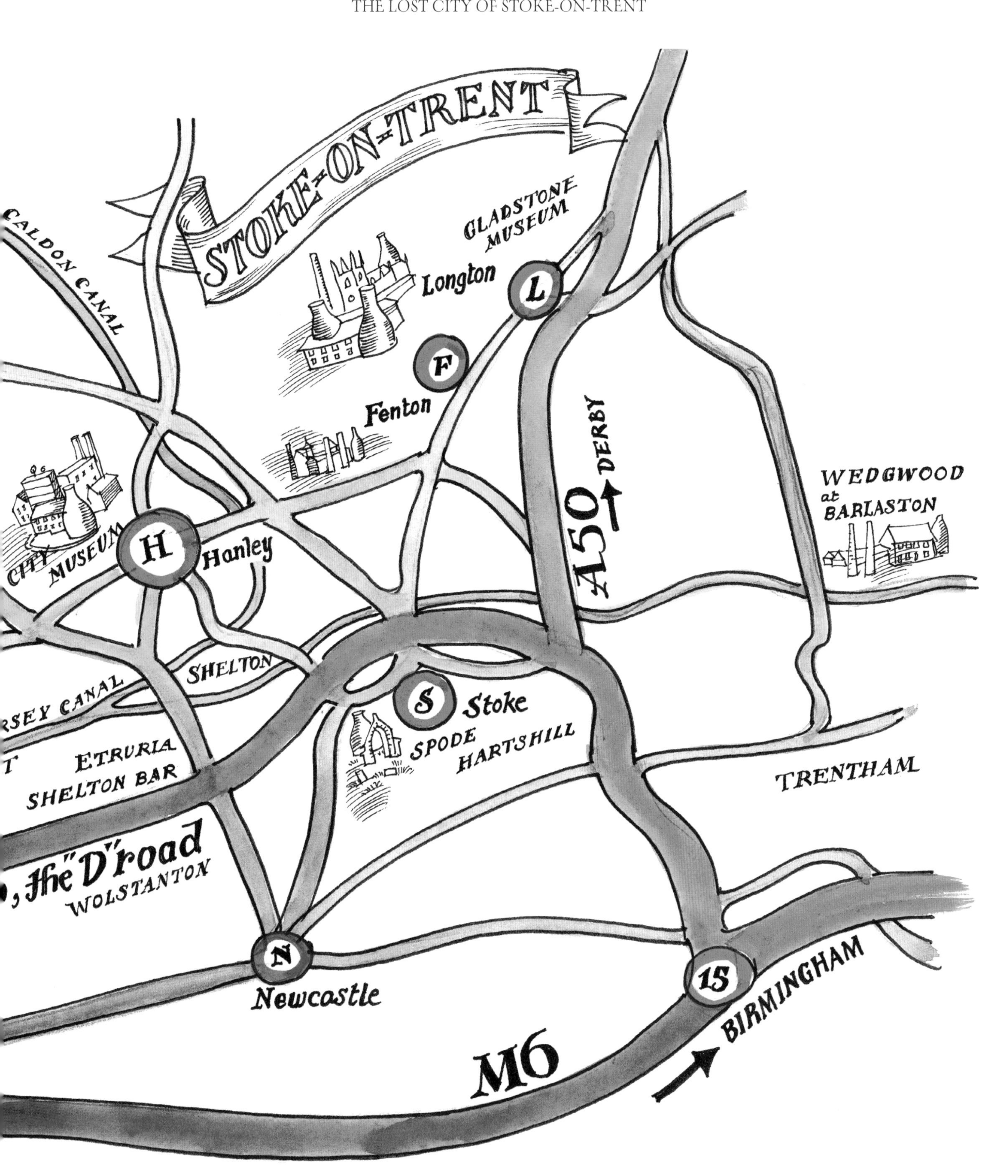
STOKE-ON-TRENT
CALDON CANAL
GLADSTONE MUSEUM
Longton
L
F
Fenton
DERBY
A50
WEDGWOOD at BARLASTON
CITY MUSEUM
H
Hanley
SHELTON
RSEY CANAL
S
Stoke
SPODE
HARTSHILL
ETRURIA
SHELTON BAR
TRENTHAM
the "D" road
WOLSTANTON
N
Newcastle
15
BIRMINGHAM
M6

THE LOST CITY

There are cities allegedly beneath the oceans, swathed in desert sands or inundated with mud, lava or volcanic dust in natural disasters. But where is Stoke-on-Trent?

Stoke is Britain's sixteenth largest city – the next largest is Cardiff – and England's twelfth biggest. It has a population of 240,000 – 350,000 if you include the neighbouring Newcastle-under-Lyme and Kidsgrove. Stoke is bang in the middle of Britain, between Birmingham, the alleged heart of England, and sexy, bustling, metropolitan Manchester. It is on the speedy and electrified west-coast Branson line and the M6, and it is surrounded by some of the most beautiful countryside in Europe. The jaw-achingly beautiful Peak District pokes its green fingers right into the city and the wide, lazy Trent valley stretches lush and pastoral to the south, while Shropshire and Cheshire are minutes away, leading on to the wilds of Wales.

Stoke should be lovely but it's not.

Stoke has all the makings of a Manchester or a Leeds: fine municipal buildings – classical, gothic or Italianate; great churches and Nonconformist chapels; 50 miles of canalside snaking through the city; and hundreds of terraces of dark, tidy, brick-built Victorian terraces.

But it is a mess.

It looks like London in 1950, as if a world war has left huge tracts of it blasted into oblivion and reconstruction is just beginning. The shopping streets make you yearn for the much-hated uniformity of the identikit high streets of the rest of England with those dreary but reliable brands. The institutes of this and that – benefactions of various Wedgwoods, Spodes or Copelands, whose industries employed the exponentially growing nineteenth-century population of the city – crumble and tumble. The churches, of eighteenth-century order or Commissioners' Gothic anonymity, are boarded against attack or have hoardings advertising trade in carpets, sofas or kitchen tiles, their churchyards truncated by ring roads, roundabouts and precincts. And everywhere is destruction, cheap and effective cleansing demolition: terraces by the dozen, factories by the dozen, chapels, chimneys and workshops, all pulverized and then left a brick-and-cement-dust desert to wait for a better plan.

The canalside factories would, in another city, have been irresistible to developers frantically keen to transform them into chic loft living. Young couples or bright young professionals would have been lured by the still ribbon of the Cauldon canal, which winds through the centre of the city, linking the wharves of long-dead manufactories with the Trent and Mersey canal, which took pottery to Manchester and Liverpool. Through those great ports of the British Empire hundreds of thousands of plates, cups and saucers, packed safely with straw in wicker crates or wooden barrels, were exported to feed markets in India and Ceylon, Argentina and Canada, Australia, America and New Zealand; in fact, the world ate off plates made in Stoke. In another city the municipal buildings would surely house parts of the two universities in Stoke: Keele, great white hope of the optimistic post-war classless society, or the new de-polyfied Staffordshire, which absorbed the last remaining of the city's five art schools. The Victorian parks, complete with bandstands, tea rooms and decorative iron railings, might be home to festivals of music or of food, perhaps, reflecting the multicultural population.

Maybe Stoke is just one industrial city too many. One more set of buildings to restore, yet another city plan to rethink, rezone and re-conceive. After all, it is alleged to be the city with the lowest quality of life in England, one of the least desirable places to live in Europe. It is a joke . . . Smoke-on-Trent (no smoke now, though: no chimneys to make it), a basket case, a hopeless situation.

The population of Stoke has, in fact, declined over the past couple of decades by about 4 per cent. It is not a healthy population: 20 per cent have a 'limiting long-term illness' (the figure nationally is 13 per cent). It also has a serious academic achievement problem. In Britain as a whole 20 per cent of the population have a degree-level qualification, whereas in Stoke 10 per cent do. Its crime levels are also higher than most and although Stoke always feels incredibly friendly, its violent crimes run at 33 per 1,000, compared to the national average of 20.

But Stoke still has the bones of a great city. There are town halls, libraries, halls and great Nonconformist temples like the Bethesda Chapel in Hanley. There are still dozens of factories and tens of thousands of artisan dwellings. There are the terraced houses that once housed the workers, larger ones for the management and still greater ones for the factory owners. Although many of these are buildings that would be valued elsewhere, in Stoke they are unloved.

Take the Villas. This is a short private road, unadopted and thus potholed and positively Third World in surface. Set back some 15 yards from this road are a set of fine stucco villas in a quiet echo of Nash's Regent's Park villas. Built for managers at Spode, these are in a dilute Italianate style that suggests the 1850s, but they were in fact a little behind the times and were built in 1878. They were designed by Charles Lynam, who was commissioned by the Stokeville Building Society, a group of prominent Stoke citizens who, wanting fine houses near but outside their town, ganged together to finance the building. The fields developed, Big Meadow and Barker's Meadow, were the property of Thomas Minton, son of the original Thomas Minton, creator of the definingly Victorian Minton pottery factory. The villas are tall and distinguished with generous eaves and round-topped windows. Steps lead up to deep porches with fanlights and elaborately tiled interiors. When one came up for sale while I was researching this book, it cost the same as a jerry-built bungalow on the edge of the city. When the excellent local paper ran an article discussing where the new chief executive of the City Council, John Van Der Laarschot, was to live the choices did not include the Villas; instead the article suggested various undistinguished suburban properties around the borough. The Villas was the first conservation area in Stoke-on-Trent, created in the 1950s, but even this did not suggest it for the role. Yet in any other city such a street would be the obvious candidate.

This is not a book about how to rescue Stoke. It contains no masterplans – there have been plenty of those – and no magic cures. The regeneration of a city is a vast and complex project. It is, however, a description of the buildings of the place, surely the raw materials with which to begin any such plan. Buildings are the physical manifestations of the characteristics of a city. Claims that a place is proud, mercantile, friendly, ancient and productive, or alternatively desperate, tired, directionless, poor and confused, are clearly supported by its built environment. The pottery factories of Stoke, for example, trumpet the extraordinary scale of the ceramics industry in a much more audible way than any number of museums. When such buildings are restored and shed their sadder memories, they can be re-used and seen in a new light. Thus they can restate the Stokishness of Stoke, even when the factories' kilns have cooled for the last time.

THE BUILDINGS OF STOKE

Cities have in common with one another certain classes of building. Early notables of the place build municipal offices, initially to define it as an up-and-coming town to be reckoned with. A market might be held under the building's elegant or more robust arches where traders from out of town – farmers, butchers and others with goods to sell – can be persuaded to congregate. These are the first steps. On the first floor will be a room in which the new town council can meet and perhaps some evidence of a concern for law and order, a lock-up and court room. All this can be small. Medieval and later examples survive: the Moot Hall in Aldeburgh, for instance, or Chipping Campden Town Hall, even the market crosses of Chichester, with a room above in which to resolve disputes about weights and measures or prices. If the commercial winds seem set fair, a larger and improved facility will quickly follow, and as municipal pomp and mercantile energy builds a head of steam the need to separate these functions into a series of purpose-built edifices arises. So the growing town will acquire a courthouse, a covered market and a town hall.

Simultaneously spiritual needs arise. The medieval church that served the original settlement becomes too small or seems inadequate in status for the new town. A larger church is built, in part to house the population at prayer on Sundays but as much to add a gloss of religion to civic life and to house the inevitable monuments to those original town hall builders as their project outlives them. The town grows and one church is not enough. It being by now the end of the eighteenth century and in the religiously free-thinking atmosphere of Great Britain, there are dissenters. Ranters and Methodists – Wesleyan, Primitive or of the New Connexion – build temples. Emancipation reveals more and more Roman Catholics, all of whom need pew space. Later Jews fleeing the pogroms of the Tsars and the poverty of the Pale of Settlement, Ugandan Asians running from the predatory and whimsical autocracy of Idi Amin or economic migrants from the jewels in the late Imperial crown all build their own places of worship.

The town grows into a city as its trade increases. It does this in Stoke's case not through trade but by manufacturing and mining. As its three great industries, coal, steel and pottery, are established, so they are housed in pits, mills and factories of ever-increasing magnitude. The proprietors of these enterprises, the great men of the city, make architectural statements with the façades of their manufactories, initially in the classical idiom and later more eclectically emphasizing their probity, power and good taste. The arrangement of a frontispiece, comprising a grand entrance as focus, becomes the norm.

That of the now demolished Hill Pottery, built for Samuel Alcock in 1839, is just such an example. It was described in Ward's directory of 1843 as 'the most striking and ornamental object of its kind within the precincts of the borough'. The factory was a fanciful stacking of classical ornament crammed together for maximum effect. A more elegant and restrained version still exists in the Boundary Works in Longton, with similar stacking of Diocletian window and open pediment above. Another, beside the wonderful Burslem Methodist Sunday School's blighted façade, is the front elevation of Wade Heath, this time of 1814. This was a format unchanged from that of Enoch Wood and Sons' Fountain Place Works in Burslem, in part restored by English Heritage. While these two survive, dozens of other factories in elegant classical clothing have been lost in the last sixty years, the most significant of these being the centrepiece, complete with bell tower to call the hands to work, of Josiah Wedgwood's Etruria. How sad that these, the best of Stoke's industrial buildings, are lost. They would, of course, now be its greatest architectural assets.

Returning to the growing city with its swiftly increasing population . . . The markets are not enough: successful tradesmen build stores and shops; visitors need accommodation; beer needs selling and must be drunk; and while the yawning days of leisure are still a way off, entertainment is needed and so theatres, music halls and later picture palaces appear.

Transport becomes a problem. The streets, rough and unmade for the early years of the city's childhood and youth, become many and long. People need to get about and more importantly so do heavy goods, by now outstretching the resources of the packhorse train. Canals are dug, followed quickly by toll roads and then more successfully by railways. All this creates buildings, stations, wharves, bridges and viaducts.

These are the civic and commercial bones of the city, in between and around which the citizens must be housed, and they are, with slight variations, common to all cities. Near the citizens' places of work, worship, supply or amusement, houses are built and rebuilt, as cheaply as possible for the workers and with increasing grace and embellishment for the more elevated classes. The owners of the businesses that fuel the city build houses that are statements of their success: some do so in the centre, as Sir Josiah Wedgwood did, building his proudly in the middle of his factory; others retire a mile or two to more sylvan spots a short drive from the belching smoke and steam.

This sounds an ordered process, one phase neatly following another, but of course this is not the case. Rather it is a jumbled race coloured by competition,

TWO DOORCASES @ St JOHN'S BURSLEM
[The graveyard contains the tomb of a renowned local WITCH ... it is now empty]
To the WEST was the CHURCHYARD WORKS where J.W. was apprenticed
JOSIAH WEDGWOOD WAS BAPTIZED HERE on the 12th JULY 1730

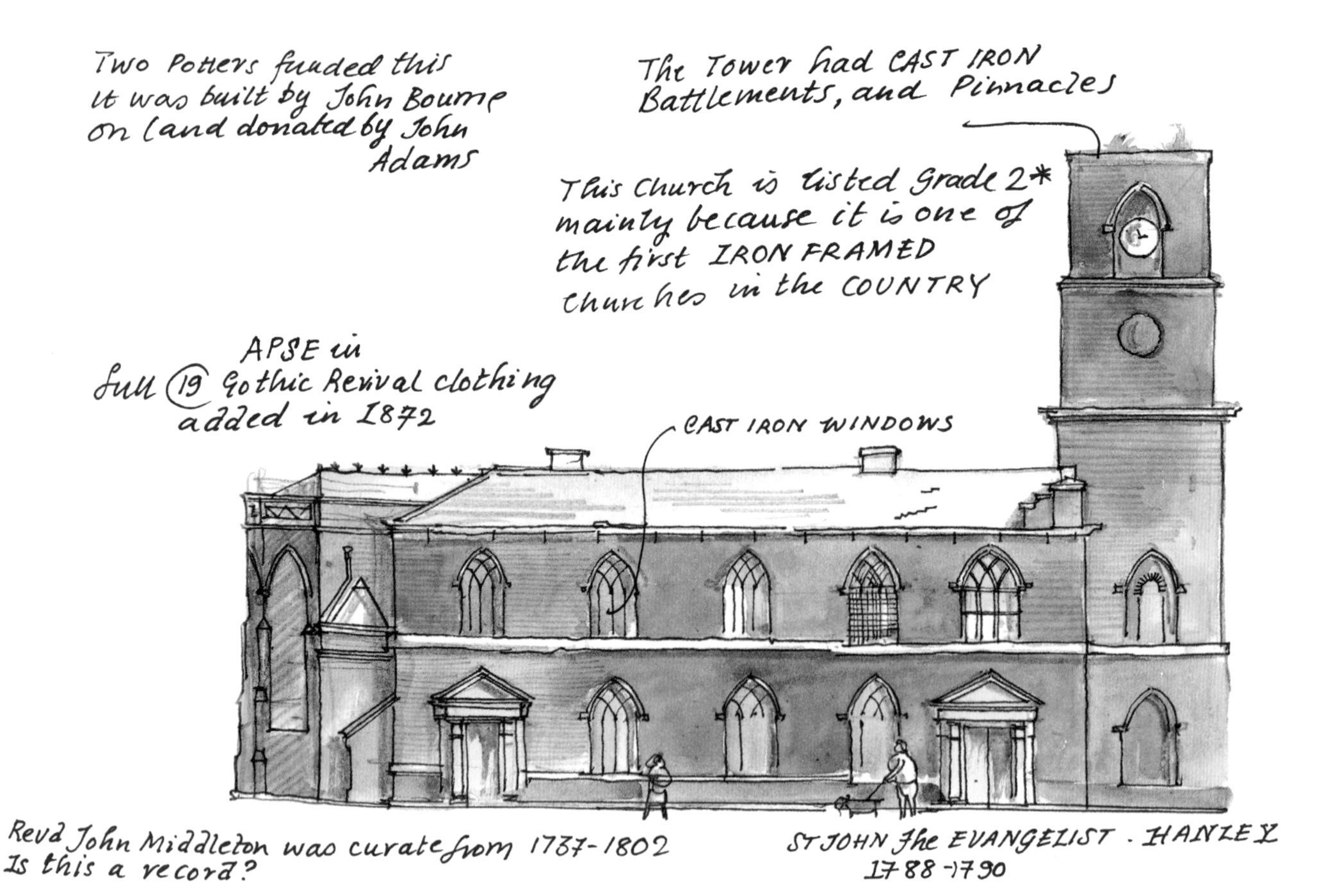

the success or failure of individuals, the vicissitudes of trade and the economy, and topographical imperatives. During its period of growth the city is self-devouring, demolishing, rebuilding and absorbing countryside. Villas in a sea of green fields that observed the factory from afar become becalmed in a stiff mass of new terraces as industry needs to house more workers and the new factory owner must build again. Mining creates gaps, huge holes and heaps or unstable land unsuited to building, and thus an industrial city takes its shape.

Stoke-on-Trent is neither an old city nor a nucleic one. Its foundation as a group of villages and later towns, leading to incorporation as a city in 1910, has given it a very characteristic, stretched-out and confusing plan. This is in great part due to the underlying geology of the place. Five of the six towns sit on a line of promontories, or little hilltops. These mark the coal seam that in the eighteenth and nineteenth centuries fuelled Stoke's industrial growth. That coal mining should entirely disappear from the city would have seemed to a resident in the 1960s, perhaps, even more unlikely than that pottery should, for until the 1990s it remained a huge employer. The names of the great pits – Chatterley Whitfield, Sneyd, Norton, Racecourse (this one at Etruria was on the site of the city's briefly thriving only racetrack, focus of much Nonconformist disapproval), Hanley Deep or Florence, named for the eldest daughter of the 3rd Duke of Sutherland, whose enterprise it was – are as redolent of Stoke's past as Minton or Spode.

The five old pottery towns (Hanley, Stoke, Longton, Burslem and Tunstall) are linked but never in a felicitous or definitive way, and while each is alleged to have particular specialities to an outside eye these are well hidden. The all-pervading air of decay is common to the whole city. While Hanley is signposted 'city centre' and contains the most convincing shopping centre, it is still hard to feel you have arrived at the heart of things; indeed, the linear and fragmented nature of the city's plan means that a drive through the middle of the area takes you not from the outer margins to the obvious centre but through a whole series of outer rings of each centre. As these outer rings are composed of warehouse sheds and other architecturally uninteresting commercial necessities, it is possible for the visitor to find the city appearing to be a perpetual suburb. In addition, a series of quite disastrous traffic management plans have left it girdled with an uncrossable and inappropriately daunting inner ring road that in effect isolates the centre of the town from its surroundings. The centre itself was subject to plenty of 1960s and 1970s rebuilding, resulting in the usual depressing poor-quality buildings replacing solid Victorian ones; and while it is currently slated for demolition, the 1970s central bus station must be a contender for grimmest building in the Midlands. Most poignant of Hanley's buildings, at its centre is an arcade of faintly Moorish precast concrete arches that connect one board-shuttered parade of shops from another, wanly light-hearted and jaunty but unloved and desperate.

Yet Hanley also contains some of the best things in Stoke. The Bethesda Chapel is a case in point. The first Bethesda Chapel was built in 1798 by the Methodist New Connexion or Kilhamites, named after their leader, Alexander Kilham from Sheffield, who had challenged the Methodist establishment and was expelled from the church in 1797. It originally held 600 seats, but these were insufficient for the observant bottoms of Nonconformist Stoke and it was enlarged, first in 1811 to seat 1,000 and then again in 1819 to hold a stonking 3,000. Behind a stucco façade with two storey'd portico there is an elegant elliptical gallery with box pews and an enormous organ towering behind the pulpit. So well attended was the chapel that all the boxes were immediately rented by the faithful, eager to show off their adherence to the movement. Indeed in 1819 only 150 seats were left 'free' and even these were rented by 1850. (It is described further on page 127.)

Opposite is the old Bluebird garage, a stylish Art Deco–Moderne building with sinuous curved elevation, recently in an exhausted state but now sensitively restored to rather more than its former glory – albeit as an all-you-can-eat-for-a-fiver oriental restaurant. Around the corner, looking on to the rear elevations of the Bethesda and its Sunday school, is the City Museum and Art Gallery, a perfectly frightful Brutalist building but with such a collection of ceramics as well as paintings, sculpture and other artefacts that you almost forgive the architect. The museum has recently played host to the extraordinary 'Staffordshire hoard', the gluttering Anglo-Saxon treasure that surfaced in 2009 in the county. Its arrival in Stoke was welcomed by two-hour queues. The MP for Stoke South for over twenty years has been Mark Fisher who, as well as representing his constituency and holding ministerial posts in the Blair government, found time to write a wonderful and invaluable guide to all the country's museums, *Britain's Best Museums and Galleries* (Penguin, 2004). His description of the museum in Hanley particularly relishes the collection of cow-shaped cream jugs given by Gabriella Keiller in the 1950s: 'a herd that numbers over six hundred, each with her number and provenance kept by Mrs Keiller in a Herd Book. The collection was given to the museum on condition that two-thirds would be displayed at any given time. They form a wall of soft-eyed, open-mouthed cows, spotty, mottled, chintzy, lustred.' Together with the Regent Theatre and the Victoria Hall the museum makes up the so-called Cultural Quarter, much heralded with brown signs and perhaps needing further attention, but a marvellous core to the city.

Of course Stoke the city has four other centres. Stoke itself, erstwhile home to the Spode pottery, is the seat of the town council, housed in a grand Victorian and Edwardian baroque palace with giant fluted columns and massive rustication. At the rear is the King's Hall of 1911, monumental and grandiose with elaborate detailing in blackened stone. The church in its first incarnation as St Peter Ad Vincula had Sir J. Wedgwood buried inside, albeit only in the porch, he not being a member of the Church of England; but demolition and the subsequent relocation of the building left him out in the cold in the churchyard. This illustrious burial alone makes Stoke another contender for king pin.

Longton is more distant but has another architecturally distinguished and distinct centre. Burslem is the oldest established town and styles itself the 'mother town'. Although especially depressed, it feels the best laid out of the centres and also has fine civic buildings. Tunstall, further out, makes the fourth centre. Fenton, the sixth town, and Shelton are significant, as are numerous lesser but distinct parts of the city, while the more genteel and secondary county-town-ish Newcastle-under-Lyme is contiguous with Stoke. Architecturally this is all very good news, as it means that Stoke has more civic buildings than any city of its size could hope to boast. And all parts of the borough have potteries: working factories and dead ones, Victorian or Regency ones and modern ones, modest workshops and whole villages of factory. All have helped to make Stoke-on-Trent an internationally known city that is still the biggest ceramic-producing city in the world.

There has been a predisposition to demolish old buildings in Stoke, either as part of a plan to redevelop this or that part of the city, or as an expedient to get rid of a problem: a gaping-windowed factory abandoned is a physical manifestation of industrial decline and the wrecker's ball comes cheap. And all over the city even now there are dinosaur corpses of the old potteries that are crumbling and therefore imperilled.

In Burslem, for example, the great Nile Street factory of Royal Doulton, established in 1877, has become a combination of brick-dust desert and a few scattered abandoned buildings. It is guarded by a sadly wrecked Art Deco gatehouse, whose curved Crittal windows follow the profile of the corner. Somehow this rather frivolous, fun-loving building, a light-hearted conceit, a last gasp of real factory architecture before the Atcost shed, the steel span and the asbestos roof replaced with pride with rude functionalism, is a particularly poignant relic. It is not listed, nor likely to become so; indeed by the time you read this it may be concrete rubble, twisted steel and broken glass. But it is significant. How many tens, hundreds of thousands of days at work started and finished at that lodge? In 1972, 7,000 people worked for Doulton across the city, 1,800 of them at Nile Street; they must almost all still be alive, so that gate must have great significance to them. Many more thousands must be dead now, but they will all have sons and daughters who went to meet their mums or dads there, saw them coming out still with a whiff of methylated spirits from their final brush cleaning and a smile for their child.

Dump the lodge and you dump the memories, collective and at the same time very personal.

We have four children, the older two born in London and the younger in Norwich. The London babies were delivered in the West London Hospital, the country ones in the Norfolk and Norwich. Both institutions have moved: the first has been absorbed by the new Chelsea and Westminster and the second removed to an out-of-town site on the edge of the city. The old sites were sold. The West London is much restored and repointed and is the home of the Ericsson mobile phone company. The maternity wing of the Norfolk and Norwich, a plain 1970s tower of ten storeys with panoramic views over the medieval city much lingered over by a generation of expectant fathers, was demolished.

When I drive around the Hammersmith Broadway roundabout and spot the plain Victorian block with its stylish logo I feel a warm glow of affection, knowing that it is where the babies came home from, where we loaded them into the car for their first trip, nervously bundling them into the unfamiliar car seat for the drive home. Why did they knock down the tower in Norwich? Isn't it the repository of thousands of happy, and sad, memories as well? Would it really have been so ill suited to conversion to a series of stylish and desirable city centre flats – in fact, might it not have made the best flats in Norwich? It is hard to make a new place, and difficult to get a development to work, yet it is very desirable to the developer to ensure that it does. Is it sensible, therefore, to chuck away the buildings, any buildings, of the past in such a careless way?

And don't we need all the cultural anchors we can grab hold of? In Stoke the lodge at Nile Street is just such a cultural anchor, and it is one of hundreds similar in the city, a physical, real, bricks-and-mortar mast to cling to, to pass every day or every week or every year, and to prompt emotions, happy and sad, that are real and not activated by posters on billboards or in shop windows.

Perhaps the orthodoxy of demolition, the bright new start and the cleansing thwack of the concrete ball – the whole idea that it might be acceptable to demolish wholesale the structure of a city in the belief, for which the evidence is surely flimsy, that it will be replaced with better – is hollow rhetoric. Of course buildings must sometimes go: some are unsafe or simply too run down to make good (ask any builder – he would always rather start afresh); some are in the wrong place, standing in the way of something greater, a new road, park or vista, and the gain from their disappearance outweighs the loss. Perhaps some, prisons or workhouses for instance, are just too sad; I would love to see the concentration camps of central Europe ground down, their sites covered in silent forest. But is the pottery industry such a bad memory? Should its heritage, its factories and warehouses and its rows of terraced houses be swept away in the name of progress? I think not.

Stoke *is* pottery. Of course it is also steel, coal, shops and offices, garages and thousands of taxis, but it is known for pottery and if it turns its back on this inheritance it is lost.

THE POTTERIES

Here is the basic technique of industrial pottery manufacture. Clay, dug locally, is mixed with more expensive but vital ingredients, principally white china clay from the West Country and, in the case of bone china, calcined bone and crushed flint. This constitutes various forms of **body**. That body is formed in various ways into shapes. This could be by **throwing** on a wheel. Or it could be by mixing with water until it has the consistency of double cream, becoming **slip**, and pouring into plaster of Paris **moulds**. This is called **slip casting**. The moisture is drawn from slip by the very absorbent plaster moulds and the piece is then taken from the mould. Alternatively the clay could be used undiluted and forced on to a revolving mould with a profiled **tool** to form the desired bowl or plate shape. This is called **jollying** or **jiggering**.

The newly made clay pieces are allowed to dry until leather hard, when they are **fettled** – that is, the rough edges and seams left by the mould are trimmed off with a steel knife and the resulting piece is **sponged** to leave a piece entirely smoothed. It is then **fired** for the first time at anything from 700 to 1100 degrees Centigrade. On emerging from the **kiln** the piece will be of the consistency of a flowerpot. This is called **biscuit ware**. It might then be decorated by painting or with a paper printed **transfer underglaze**; or perhaps **glazed** first by dipping in **glaze**, a solution of minerals that when **fired** again, this time at 900–1300 degrees Centigrade, will form a smooth glassy surface to the pot. It could then be decorated **onglaze**; or, if the colour or **transfer** is to melt right into the glaze, **inglaze**; or, if prior to glazing, **underglaze**. Some very elaborate ware is painted and fired repeatedly in layers with **enamel** colours. Thus a cup might have been fired twice or as many as six times.

The body may be **earthenware**, red or various shades of cream to white; or it may be more vitreous, **stoneware** or **porcelain**, although the recipe for the latter has always remained more a Continental one. The introduction in the late eighteenth century of calcined bone produced the hard and bluey white **bone china**, which replaced cream earthenware as the required body for formal dinnerware and ruled supreme for 150 years.

The bone in question makes up about 50 per cent in weight of the final clay body recipe. Any meat still adhering to the bone is removed (and sold as pet food). Then the bone is treated to remove whatever can go to make glue – that is, the collagen, which also is used for sizing expensive paper. What is left gets heated to 1000 degrees Centigrade and any remaining organic material is burned away. The inorganic compounds found in bone are, of course, rich in calcium. This is in the form of calcium phosphate, which makes up about 50 per cent of bone.

The original basic formula for bone china of six parts bone ash (calcined bone), four parts china stone and three and a half parts china clay remains the standard body. Hard porcelain is strong but chips fairly easily and, unless specially treated, is usually tinged with blue or grey. Bone china is easier to manufacture, is strong, does not chip easily and has an ivory-white appearance. Following its introduction the potters of Stoke opted for this body and this has remained the case until the present day.

Stoke-on-Trent means pottery. It is known as the Potteries in the way that Detroit is called Motown. Such an overriding connection with its principal product is rare. Northampton made shoes but it was never called the Booteries; Hull manufactured paint and maintained a huge fishing fleet but it has no secondary name that alludes to this. Perhaps this equation is because without pots Stoke is nothing, unlike Northampton, a county town, or Hull, a great port with medieval origins. It is rather a group of Staffordshire villages whose geological situation above easily accessible deposits of clay and coal made it the perfect place to make and fire pottery.

Every village in pre-industrial Britain made pottery. As in present-day India, the village potter with a wood- or charcoal-fuelled kiln would produce the basic wares needed for life: bowls, beakers and jugs, storage vessels and cooking pots. These kilns would be fired weekly and the smashed failures discarded close by in a heap to be discovered centuries later in archaeological digs.

Broken pottery is a good find. It is like coins, in that we all know what it is; the rim of a bowl or mug, the handle of a jug or the three-footed base of a cooking pot are recognizable parts of our own daily lives. There is somehow a more accessible thrill to finding a glazed fragment of a jug than an incomprehensible post hole, and while not date-stamped in the way that a coin is, pottery is still easily dated.

I live in Oxford and behind our house is Port Meadow, a large expanse of grass, frequently flooded. It is a wonderful piece of open space, frequented in the winter by the most romantic and wild waders and wildfowl: godwits and golden plover, shovellers and pintails, with a whistling soundtrack of wigeon, ducks who have spent the summer glamorously in Siberia or Scandinavia. However, about 30 acres of the meadow nearest to the railway line never flood. But sepia photographs of the mid-nineteenth century show little clinker-built dinghies sailing all over this area, then known as the Refuge. In the 1870s the place became a rubbish dump for expanding Oxford's domestic refuse. This Victorian landfill project left that land several feet higher than it was before and it was to flood as the Refuge no longer. Today notices warn against the damage caused by bottle digging. Closer investigation of the ruffled

Blue & White engraved Jug 1830-40

meadow turf reveals a sprinkling of scraps of pottery, stoneware jars, earthenware fragments and handles – indeed even a few pieces of spongeware. The Oxford Union Canal runs parallel to the railway and no doubt carried those teapots and plates from Stoke to Oxford in the nineteenth century.

A similar archaeological thrill may also be had at Stoke. But in contrast, a Stoke dig will yield a far richer harvest, as factories and houses were frequently built on foundations entirely constructed of shraff, or fired pottery waste. Even the rankest of amateurs spotting a building site beside the road can quickly achieve a representative view of the city's output at any particular date.

Some potters must have had a nattier way with pulling mug handles or a particular style of decoration that made their wares desirable beyond their immediate neighbourhood. There had always been imported pieces – Rhenish wares from Germany, grey and blue stoneware, became popular in England from the fourteenth century onwards, with trade peaking in the sixteenth century, and coloured glazed faience from Italy or France, in the seventeenth century. But transport was such a problem until the nineteenth century that all but the highest-status goods were made as close to their eventual home as possible; most ceramic objects in domestic use were made within 10 miles of their place of use.

The Industrial Revolution, however, changed everything. The growing population lived a deracinated urban life, their village lives abandoned and the village trades becoming marginalized. Farmers may have travelled to market in the emerging industrial towns to sell food, but the hardware of life was made in town. The scale of manufacture grew exponentially, too, and, as this happened, power and finding fuel for it became the challenge. When coal fired the great bottle kilns that so characterized the urban landscape of Stoke-on-Trent of the past, it took eight times as much coal as clay to make a pot. Thus proximity to the source of that coal was of paramount importance.

As it always had been. The north Staffordshire coalfields, centred around the small towns of Burslem, Tunstall and Longton, were close to the surface and consequently easy and cheap to mine. On maps you can see the coal and clay pits right in among the city. Before 1700 potters were publicly criticized for digging holes in roads to get at the clay – a practice that (according to the Stoke-on-Trent City Council, who may be thought to have an interest) resulted in the term 'potholes'. The local clay, Etruria marl, was also plentiful and easily extracted. A fledgling industry developed at the end of the seventeenth century with master potters who excelled, whose wares went beyond the everyday.

In the City Museum in Hanley there is an earthenware jug in the shape of an owl, dated very roughly 1660–1730 and called Ozzy. It is dark brown and the plumage is rendered in a decorative technique called slipware, in which liquid clay, or slip, provides the colours. The liquid clay is trailed on to the body, like cake icing. A comb-like implement is used to mix the colours together, producing a marbled effect. The pot is then glazed and fired and the contrast between the various coloured slips becomes exaggerated. In the case of Ozzy the head comes off and forms a cup. This owl is no everyday trinket: it is a serious decorative piece, a wedding present or a birthday tribute to a mother, perhaps? The technique of slipware is particularly well suited to writing. In neighbouring display cases at the museum there are more examples of this sort of ware: platters, jugs and a hefty three-handled mug, or posset pot, one plate bearing the legend 'The Best Is Not Too Good For You'. The piece is signed 'Thomas Toft 1700'. He is our first named master potter in Stoke.

The name Toft has been found prominently marked on numerous slipware dishes of the late seventeenth and early eighteenth centuries. The Christian name is most commonly Thomas, but also Ralph, who may have been his son or his brother. Around 30 Thomas Toft dishes and 17 attributed to Ralph Toft are known to exist; 11 of the Ralph ones are in museums and one sold for $114,000 in January 2006. We also know of a Cornelius Toft and a James Toft, but it is by no means certain that someone named Toft made all the dishes that say Toft. It is more likely that the Toft style became so popular that other potters began to put the name on their own work, creating simply a 'Toft style'. The designs are of mermaids, cavaliers, pelicans and sometimes Charles II drawn on in red, brown and black, with a cross-hatched border.

Of Thomas Toft's contemporary Thomas Wedgwood we know little beyond his having been similarly employed and living in Burslem from 1687 to 1739, dying when

DECORATIVE PLATE made by Tost brothers. They had a factory at TINKERSCLOUGH (clough = lane) in what would become ETRURIA

LEAD-GLAZED EARTHENWARE with TRAILED SLIP DECORATION

his youngest child, Josiah, was nine years old. (He was Thomas Wedgwood III, the son of Thomas Wedgwood II.) We do know, however, that Josiah was born in 1730 and that as a young man he had premises in the Churchyard pottery beside Burslem parish church. Sixty-five years later Josiah was buried to universal eulogy and sadness at the parish church of Stoke. He was a fellow of the Royal Society, a knight of the realm, father-in-law to the youthful Charles Darwin and pottery manufacturer by appointment to the Queen; and he had been the principal player in turning the ceramic industry into one of Britain's greatest, employing 25,000 workers.

With his contemporaries Thos Wheildon (1719–95), the great master potter of Shelton, and another Josiah, J. Spode (1733–97), he had changed the output of those Midlands kilns from redware teapots, slipware plates and crude tin and salt-glazed pieces to a baffling range of ceramics: Queen's ware, creamware, caneware, pearlware, basaltware, jasperware and countless other variations of body and decorative effect. His early joint enterprises with Wheildon had developed the well-known naturalistic cauliflower-shaped teapots and leafy plates with coppery green glazes, but from then on he used a variety of shapes and styles. At the height of his career he was looking far beyond the Potteries for his inspiration.

The meteoric growth of Wedgwood's business was inextricably linked with the phenomenon of the Grand Tour, adopted in the eighteenth century as a *de rigueur* part of the upbringing of an aristocratic young gent. The path from London was well known . . .

A fantasy

Across the Channel via the great cathedrals of northern France, a crashing hangover in Rheims, a winsome waitress in Chartres necessitating a speedy departure from that city. An unforgettable month in the hotels of pre-Haussmann Paris and a sight of Louis at Versailles, a nervous two days when it seemed that Father had not forwarded funds for the second part of the journey and then with a sigh of relief the heavy carriage continuing south, veering east to admire, and then experience a little too closely, the Romantic glories of the Alps, already perceived as a rugged marvel and not just a practical horror to be overcome. A dull three days with the serious-minded burghers of Geneva. A blissful day's picnic on an alpine meadow waving blue with gentians and flecked with waxy white edelweiss, lying reading Fielding on that tight sward in the cool mountain air and thinking how far removed it seemed from the dark Tudor rooms of the great manor house in Dorset from which the journey began three months earlier. Mother weeping and uttering dire threats about Italian brigands – her own lurid literary fantasy perhaps? Father, would he *never* drop that irksome taint of the West Country in his slow deliberate farewell?

The PORTLAND VASE. (Was property of D. of P. in 1780s)

J. WEDGWOOD COPIED this from one discovered near Rome in 1625.

The first was made in Stoke in 1790.

The early trials (in the Wedgwood museum) are instructive . . .

And the next morning waking in Aosta, a new language and one that Dr Langland's interminable Latin lessons at the hall had made faintly familiar through its garbled chatter and a new lightness. A new Italian guide wearing a London coat of antiquated cut and of a colour last seen in St James's ten years before, no doubt the gift of an earlier milord, hurries through the arcaded streets, his description tantalizingly close to being understandable – the fluency will come, Arthur, wait another month and it will soak in with the southern sun – and suddenly there it is, Hadrian's Arch, gaunt and grey, simplified and stripped of its decorated marble casing, but, the breeched young traveller knows, it is only a primitive whispered forerunner of the treats to come in the Roman Forum. Continuing south, leaving behind the vine-striped hillsides unchanged since Virgil saw them nearly two thousand years earlier . . .

Edward Gibbon drily noted: 'According to the law of custom, and perhaps of reason, foreign travel completes the education of an English gentleman.'

Why am I going on about this Grand Tourist? Where does it fit in? Surely the trip does not include Stoke-on-Trent? Wait a bit longer . . .

He arrives to stay for a month with Count Emo in his villa in the Veneto. His noble forebear, the admiral through whose bold and decisive action at Chioggia in 1380 the Serenissima itself was saved from the ravages of the grand Turk, was inspired by his friends to commission Andrea Palladio to design a house in the middle of his productive agricultural estate on the mainland. It is here that we leave our hero, pacing the arcaded loggia as the warm May rain falls on the freshly clipped box and bay hedges, listening to the low trilling of a daytime nightingale and wondering how he can ever return to basic and unlovely England, and vowing that when he does (he must, as he is to marry the uneducated but doe–eyed heiress from the neighbouring valley) it will be to make his life there an imitation as close as possible to the eye-opening heaven he is presently inhabiting.

This Grand Tourist is my invention, his travels my fantasy. Readers searching for a much fuller account of a

Various 18 STAFFORDSHIRE FIGURES · Being early they are three dimensional · Later, & Cheaper, versions were "Flat back" like the ubiquitous spaniels

1780

J. WOOD 1780-1800

real trip could do no better than to read *Arbiter of Elegance: A Biography of Robert Adam* by Roderick Graham, the story of the architectural giant of the late eighteenth-century Robert Adam, whose three-year version, starting in 1754, affected not only his own home and tastes but those of his whole country. But my Tourist is a type and a significant one in Georgian England.

For what does he do at home to reclaim the lost dream of Italy? He – and his companions and peers and imitators – develop, to a fine degree, a taste for the classical, for the visual language of the ancients and for objects of vertu that are forever reminders of that life-changing trip. Thus with the Enlightenment and fuelled financially by the increasingly powerful economy of the world's first industrialized nation came a great change in sophisticated middle-class tastes (indeed the very idea of a middle class was beginning to develop at this time).

The early potters were on to this and their products changed, their designs absorbing and reflecting these new values and tastes. Classical urns, lamps and jugs and many smaller and more useful vessels in imitation of those forms were thrown, turned and cast in the new model factory that Josiah Wedgwood erected at Shelton on the edge of Hanley in 1769. He called it Etruria, a compelling name referring to the proto-Roman culture of central Italy just then coming to the attention of the antiquarian, and one calculated to recommend it and its wares to the newly cultured and refined Englishman of classical tastes.

Etruria was more than a pottery. Housing was provided for the workers, and warehousing and grinding mills for the flint and china stone that had become such a vital part of the new methods of production that Wedgwood was developing. And standing grandly above this conglomeration was Etruria Hall, the seat of Sir J., austere and imposing and such an advertisement of the taste of its builder that he had a road diverted and replaced with a smart new toll road, down which visitors to the works would arrive, in perfect alignment with this phenomenon.

Wedgwood did not work in a vacuum. While he was testing and testing again the new ceramic bodies and ever more sophisticated glazes that would characterize his ware, Enoch Wood and Ernest Davenport in nearby Burslem, and Josiah Spode in Stoke, along with a growing band of lesser potters, were establishing an industry that would supply the world.

Early potters did not backstamp their wares. The neat little corporate badges, the diamonds and ribbons and escutcheons printed, painted or impressed on the bases

VARIOUS URNS of the CLASSICAL PERSUASION, MARBLEWARE or BASALT with SPRIGGED and MOULDED DECORATION LATE 18

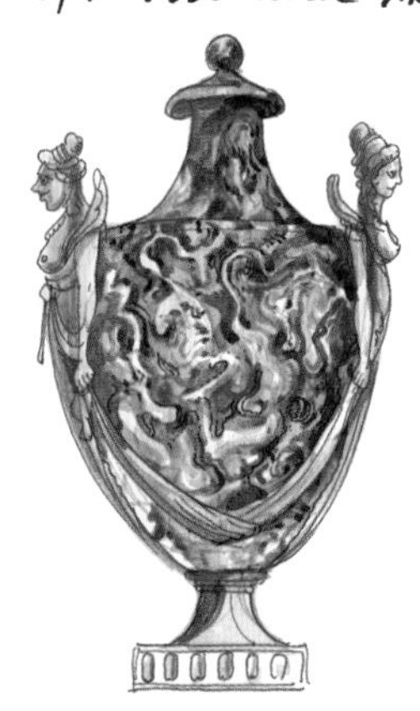

of most Victorian plates, often with optimistic armorial pretensions, were a late addition to the industry. This makes early pieces hard to pin down to their place of manufacture and any such assignment must be an educated guess. However, from the 1850s onwards it became standard practice in all but the lowliest establishments to backstamp each piece made and it is possible to trace most pieces to a site in the city, though very few of these are still the homes of potteries.

Both Josiahs realized that presenting their highly worked pottery to the correct market was every bit as important as its actual manufacture. Wedgwood set up grand glass-cased premises in Piccadilly, while Spode went into partnership with Mr Copeland in a London emporium of their own. In due course the latter became the stronger man and the Copeland family controlled Spode until 1966.

The aim of the early potters was, in turning their back on the earthy tones and textures of native ware, to imitate as closely as possible the pearly white porcelain of the Orient. Attempts had been made to imitate this from the fifteenth century onwards, but the composition was not understood. Initial experiments used mixtures of clay with ground-up glass or sand to try to achieve the original's lightness and translucency, but these suffered and became misshaped in the kiln and were uneconomic on a large scale. Imports of china became much more frequent in the seventeenth century to accompany the tea-drinking craze and so the incentive to produce a porcelain-like ware that could compete with these became great. (Louis XIV, the Sun King, built a tiled pavilion for his mistress, Madame de Montespan, called the Trianon de Porcelaine, although it was in fact made of tin-glazed earthenware. Alas, the tiles would fracture and fall off in cold weather and Mme de M. fell out of favour. The Trianon was destroyed in 1687.)

White porcelain was made at Meissen from 1713 and from 1740 at Sèvres with a royal warrant. France and Italy continue to vie as to who was the initiator of European porcelain manufacture. The compositions of these wares was a secret as closely guarded as the recipe for Coca-Cola is today. Understandably, no one was telling anyone else exactly how they were making it.

In Stoke various materials were all crushed and employed to both harden and lighten the colour of the pots – china clay from Cornwall and Devon, feldspar from Derbyshire, flint from the south coast and later bone – in the search for a durable porcelain body, first successfully achieved at Longton Hall in 1751. China clay and the china stone from Cornwall are not exactly the same as the kaolin and the feldspathic and micaceous petuntse used in Chinese porcelain, but they do contain feldspar and mica, as well as some quartz, kaolinite and fluorite – a mineral better known in its guise of the shiny purple-blue and yellow crystally stone Blue John.

Wedgwood himself developed a cream earthenware so buttery pale and thin that he was able to persuade Queen Charlotte, wife of George III, both to commission a service of it and to lend to it the commercially enticing name Queen's ware. This became extraordinarily successful. It too was the result of a process of experimentation which centred around the use of Cornish china clay. This was severely hindered by a patent taken out by a Cornishman Richard Campion. Such protectionism was the bane of the Staffordshire potteries and Wedgwood set out to prevent an extension of this patent. He went to Cornwall with John Turner.

Turner had been in business in Longton (then called Lane End) since 1762 and had himself discovered a desirable vein of peacock marl, a clay capable of producing pale-coloured ware. The Turner–Wedgwood trip was a success and with the exception of a prohibition on the manufacture of translucent porcelain Stoke had access to the Duchy's china clay. The remaining restriction was lifted in 1796 and the development of the china industry began in earnest.

The early 1800s (from *c.*1797 onwards) saw the introduction of bone china, a harder and less fragile ware with, unsurprisingly, a high proportion of calcined bone in its make-up. Some calcined bone had been used since the 1750s, but it was Spode in the late 1790s who made the breakthrough in the production of bone china.

While it took 8 tons of coal to produce 1 ton of earthenware pottery, for bone china the amount of coal rose to 17 tons because the firing temperature is higher, at 1200 degrees Centigrade (Cornwall, despite containing the UK's only deposits of china stone, conveniently for Stoke and its emerging ascendancy as premier ceramic manufacturing centre of Britain has no coal). However, existing methods and ovens could be used. The sequence of processes required for firing, enamelling, glazing and so on was pretty much the same as that for earthenware, so easy to adapt to. Another advantage of bone china is that the firing temperature is lower than that used for hard-paste porcelain – 1250 as opposed to 1400 degrees Centigrade – and so not as much coal is needed. It is also less liable to loss in firing than porcelain bodies that contained feldspar. Hence it became the ubiquitous English china.

Concurrently with the development of this highest-status show-off flourish, more everyday wares with simple floral painted borders began to fill the parlours of the more refined farmhouses and tradesmen's homes. The reigns of George III and IV and William IV, and the first ten years of Victoria's, saw an extraordinary flowering of production: borders ever more elegant or surprisingly bold and shapes refined but practical and peculiarly well suited to the fine-cast cream earthenware of the age.

The new technology collided with the mid-nineteenth century's indecision about whither architectural styles should proceed. Pugin's gothic, Nash's picturesque, Barry's Italianate or Cockerell's exuberant late classicism? Ceramics, like all applied arts, followed architecture and while the theorists floundered in a mire of gothic tracery and cornices and architraves the potters wandered blindly around as well. Shapes became absurdly exaggerated or weirdly mannered and decoration stiffer and ever more reliant on heavy gold. Raised and textured borders and unlovely pattern, elaborate for its own sake, conspired to make meretricious and heavy-handed ware of little charm. This elaboration and lack of design focus was common to all manufacturers – from Spode, Wedgwood and Minton to the lowliest back-street pottery – who, at this time as at any other, were inclined to follow one another's design innovations.

At the lower end of the scale, however, kitchen wares and pottery for the expanding world of the railways and hotels retained a more convincing authority, and as Britain became yet further industrialized so a more

industrial pottery was produced. Stoneware, the famous Mason's ironstone and other utilitarian wares were loaded on to the barges for the canal trip to Manchester, Liverpool or London. The cheapest ware of all, low-fired poor-quality earthenware, was decorated as quickly and cheaply as possible, under the glaze to save firing, often with the cut roots of sponges. This spongeware, characterized by the use of repeating patterns of geometrical or natural forms in bold, cheap, colours, was used in the most ordinary of kitchens or packed tightly with straw in wooden barrels and exported to the distant colonies – India, Ceylon, South and East Africa and beyond. This was an export market that worked and saw the industry grow to its zenith in the lush years before the Great War of 1914–18.

Countless factories opened and closed as one or another potter rose from the factory floor to overseer, manager and then master, only to tumble again, blighted by the vicissitudes of world trade or by his own unrealistic ambitions. Potteries of any sort have never been very secure businesses. Even in the eighteenth century they were often short-lived enterprises that fell as the owners' partnerships began to fracture. The great Sir J.W. himself went into four separate business marriages, as did many of his contemporaries. When great pottery owners sold their business interests, the businesses frequently failed to thrive under their new ownership.

Export was both a destroyer of hopes and a maker of fortunes. The promise of unexploited markets of untold wealth in the newly independent United States wove a particularly efficacious spell over many potters and it was no chimera. Indeed from the 1750s onwards the then colony of Virginia and its key trading cities, Philadelphia and Boston, with their growing rival New York began to solidify as significant markets for the ceramic producers of Stoke. In 1765 Wedgwood wrote to Sir William Meredith (MP for Liverpool and general champion of the interests of the colony against the hard-taxing and unsympathetic government of Westminster):

The bulk of our particular manufacture are, you know, exported to foreign markets, for our home consumption is very trifling compared to what is sent abroad; and the principal of these markets are the Continent and Islands of N. America. To the Continent we send an amazing quantity of white stoneware and some of the finer kinds but for the islands we cannot make anything too rich and costly.

There are many records surviving of sales and auctions. For example, in Charleston in 1797 the March edition of the *City Gazette* announces:

Imported on the ship Ruby. Captain Smith. From London. 29 Hogshead well assorted Staffordshireware. It consists of the greatest variety of useful articles, blue china, blue and green edge and plain yellow ware with Tea pots, bowls, basins etc and by the reason of the invoice not arriving with the ship, it now lies in the Custom House warehouse . . .

Meanwhile Mr Lees, a Liverpool merchant who dealt with the American market and was in regular receipt of deliveries of earthenware from J. Wedgwood, exported in March 1806:

30 crates table plates
10 crates supper plates
10 crates twiflers and muffins
5 crates dishes
5 crates baking dishes and sallads
5 crates turrines, sauce boats and fancy ware
30 crates assorted and small things

A modern-day manufacturer would be delighted to dispatch an order so big (and so approximate in detail – although perhaps he would have difficulty supplying sufficient twiflers).

Certain political events had significant effects on the America trade. Perhaps surprisingly, the revolution of 1776 was not the greatest of these, although the civil war had a clear effect. Restrictions on trade – basically the real risk of attack on enemy merchant shipping in the

↓ MOCHAWARE JUG

This very characteristic C19 decorative technique was particularly popular for pub tankards

The TREE-LIKE motifs were FORMED by DRIPPING a MIXTURE of URINE & TOBACCO onto unfired slip.....

EARTHENWARE JUG MID C19 B+WHITE TRANSFER WARE

WEDGWOOD JUG 1790

IMPLORING FIGURE OF A SLAVE. 1830. The ANTI-SLAVERY MOVEMENT made this kind of mode V. POPULAR

Lt HUGH MONRO was killed in India (by a tiger) in 1792 This is an earthenware model commemorating this 1815–1820

* A wooden model also exists in the form of an ORGAN (also in the V&A. Museum)

CREAMWARE JUG
EARLY (19)

CREAMWARE TEA JAR
1760-80

1723 POSSET POT
(POTTERIES MUSEUM
STOKE.)

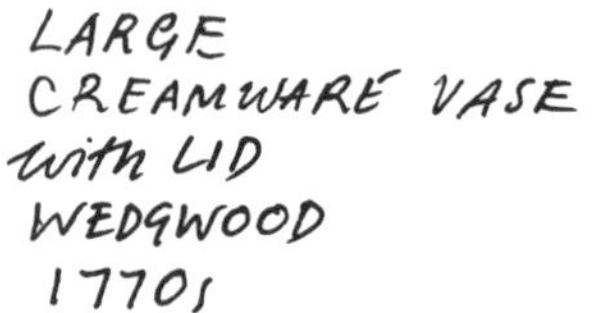

LARGE
CREAMWARE VASE
with LID
WEDGWOOD
1770s

POSSET POT 1740 - 1760
REDWARE with SPRIGGING

SPRIGGING IS PRESS-MOULDED
APPLIED DECORATION

CANEWARE TEAPOT in the form of Bamboo. MID C18 WEDGWOOD

EARLY C18 PORCELAIN TEAPOT

SLIPWARE TANKARD 1725.

TWO CREAMWARE TEAPOTS

C 1850

C 1950

Atlantic throughout the period – relating to the Anglo–American wars of 1812–14 (which had themselves arisen partially in reaction to restrictions imposed by Britain on US/French trade) were just such a snarl-up. Stoke felt the consequent cessation of business keenly, although such wares as were already in the United States benefited from immediate rises in price because of their scarcity. This was only a temporary advantage to the American traders. John C. Abbott of New Jersey wrote with the characteristic pragmatism of the tradesman, 'there is a vast quantity of English goods not to be had for love nor money – queens ware exceedingly high . . . now none to be had, other things in proportion. This country, as well as England feels the want of free commercial intercourse.'

The export market imposed certain requirements on the Staffordshire factories. The increased costs of shipping had to be passed on to the transatlantic customer, who was himself characterized by the nature of his relatively young country. In 1790 90 per cent of the population were employed on the land, and by 1800 that figure was still 70 per cent. Their low wages precluded the purchase of 'fancy goods' from Stoke. There was, of course, an established gentry class, indeed even a proto-aristocracy on the east coast, but this represented a small proportion of the market as a whole. Although for them products were of a similar level of sophistication as those available in London, orders comprised in the great part affordable everyday wares, bordered, engraved, banded or sponged and some just plain coloured. It was common practice to pass on seconds or even third-quality wares to this price- but not necessarily quality-conscious market. In 1809 Richard Shaw, merchant of Stoke, agreed to purchase all the 'thirds cream coloured ware' produced by Wedgwood and Byerley for export to America (here means third-quality ware).

At this early stage, the eighteenth and early nineteenth centuries, little or no attention was paid to originating 'American' designs for everyday use, although Wedgwood and others had produced commemorative wares bearing the likeness of Washington, Adams, Franklin and other key figures, and indeed events, of the early years of the new United States. However, a spirit of competition between manufacturers and the very real threat of the import of French porcelain, stylish but cheap, caused this to change. A taste in the cities of the eastern seaboard for the elegant white wares of France was quickly observed and built upon, and shapes and ware in imitation were swiftly and opportunistically put into production in Staffordshire. John Edwards of Fenton produced a tureen in 1879 that was so close in design to one registered only three years earlier by C.F. Havilland of Limoges (France's equivalent ceramic capital) that the French company successfully sued. Bridgwood's porcelain opaque ware was actually advertised by Woodward and Phelps, dealers in china in Park Place, New York, as being 'a close imitation of white French China in shape, weight and finish'. The advertisement continues to state that its cost is but 'a trifle more than ordinary white granite'.

White granite, or white ironstone, was a hardwearing low-cost body, cheap to produce and easy to transport, that was the staple mid-nineteenth-century US export ware. It was unique in that it was a ceramic body perceived as being not only suitable for export to the States but specifically unsuitable to sales at home. Whole factories in Stoke were dedicated to its manufacture and these were particularly susceptible to downturns in the American trade. It was predominantly left undecorated, either with moulded decoration but sometimes with applied or surface pattern. The cunningly named John Wedge Wood, who was a potter of Burslem from the 1830s until 1857 (and the business was continued by his brother until 1876 at Tunstall), devoted his entire enterprise to the American trade.

He was also remarkable in that his sales were not restricted to Boston, Philadelphia and New York. During the middle years of the nineteenth century the great push west across the virgin prairie lands of the American continent began in earnest. This was initiated by the

The language of CLASSICAL ORNAMENT reigned supreme in the late 18

Louisiana purchase of 1803, and with the acquisition of the Oregon territory in 1846, the annexation of the Texan Republic in 1845 and the gains from the Mexican wars that ended in 1848 the country realized roughly its current boundaries. Lands to settle meant farmsteads to be built and kitchens to fill with the vital, and ceramic, goods of everyday life.

The Americans themselves were frequently put out by the assumption that they would absorb whatever pottery was thrown at them, perhaps rightly, as the Staffordshire press was quite outspoken about how carelessly omnivorous the American consumer was likely to be. Benjamin Franklin, one of the founding fathers of the USA, wrote in 1789 to Mr Wright, a banker, commenting on this. John Ward in *The Borough Of Stoke-upon-Trent* paraphrased the letter:

English merchants acted imprudently in forcing such quantities of goods on the Americans, which had not been ordered by them, and were beyond the facilities of their country to consume in any reasonable time; and the surplus of which was, therefore, sent to vendues, or auction-houses, where it was frequently sold for less than the prime cost, to the great loss of the indiscreet adventurers.

In Franklin's words: 'I see in your newspapers frequent mention made of our being out of credit with you; to us, it appears we have abundantly too much, and that your exporting merchants are rather out of their senses!'

Perhaps this assumption that the output of the Staffordshire potteries would inevitably find a market continued until the end of the twentieth century, when it finally became clear that manufacturers could no longer force their wares on an increasingly sophisticated customer, whether in Britain, America or further afield.

The production of all these wares necessitated not only the establishment of potteries – potbanks in the vernacular – but also several ancillary industries: flint mills, bone mills, paper mills, printers (these last two for the production of the engraved transfers so popular from the late eighteenth century), colour and glaze makers, kiln builders and so on. One of the finest and best preserved of the kilns is the Jesse Shirley Flint Mill, now the Etruria Industrial Museum, where great Welsh chert stones are driven round by wooden paddles crushing bone or flint. Such enterprises characterized the landscape of Stoke-on-Trent from its beginning until the collapse of the industry in the 1990s. Their chimneys and bottle kilns, the long two- or three-storey factories some twenty or more bays long, often with wings or further fingers of factories attached, the grandiose gatehouses and lodges, which like the frontispiece or Tower of the Orders in the middle of an Elizabethan or Jacobean prodigy house allude to the alleged fine taste and sophistication of the owners of the factory – all these were the stuff of Stoke. As were the thousands of pottery workers employed in the factories.

While these enterprises provided work, it was not always very pleasant. There were obviously health risks involved in this very manual industry. The use of lead glazes was banned in 1948, putting an end to the horrifyingly debilitating affliction of 'potter's rot', which was virtually passed from father to son, as it was customary to work alongside your family, using them as inexpensive assistants. Since then there have been no lead-related deaths. Pollution was a problem, particularly in the days of coal-fired bottle kilns. The sun was often virtually blacked out by smoke; people still remember walking down the street and being unable to see the person walking beside them. There were very high levels of diseases of the lungs, respiratory problems and the like, resulting in a high death rate. The Clean Air Act of 1956 dealt with this and increasing regulation of the environment both inside and outside the factory, while perhaps making the city less picturesque, ensured that it was a healthier and better place to live.

A factory that has survived almost unchanged is Burgess and Leigh in Middleport, a canalside corner of Burslem. This factory, or complex of industrial buildings, provides a glimpse of nineteenth-century England. Burgess and Leigh was never a top-flight manufacturer. Its wares – transfer-decorated tea services and other inexpensive pottery for the small farmhouse, the suburban villa or the park keeper's cottage – were pretty and down to earth. Sprigged with blue and white flowers or views, hand banded, or finished, in dozens of decorative Victorian shapes, the output of this factory was frequently exported or sold by dealers in market stalls throughout the country. At its peak it employed 700 people in long workshops that were, in 1888, advanced and modern manufacturing facilities.

The then current practice of isolating each function into a separate workshop was exemplified in this plan. It was a system widely adopted and had been recommended a century earlier by Josiah Wedgwood, both to avoid wasteful interdepartmental chatter and as an attempt to maintain trade secrets. Thus access to the upper floors was gained by outdoor stairs and the whole grid of buildings was divided by yards, wide enough for ventilation and security but close enough to avoid pointless moving around of ware. A splendid coal-fired boiler operated what was at the time a highly mechanized system in which moulds were dried in a mangle dryer, a power-driven column 30 feet high. The assembly of long ranges of three-storey workshops was interspersed with bottle kilns and chimneys. Its architectural focus is, as usual, the gatehouse. Being a late nineteenth-century factory it does not follow the 'Venetian window over the depressed arch' format of the early factories. Rather the gate itself sits beneath a gothic arch, simple in structure but much embellished with decorative brickwork – not unlike four other gables that punctuate the façade.

Passing beneath the arch one enters the nineteenth century. A springy weighbridge that once checked the loads of horse-drawn vehicles lies before a film set of an office. Near-Dickensian high desks, an ancient Marmoleum floor and portraits of grim-faced Leighs staring forward from the full-bearded 1890s to the thin-tied 1950s gaze mournfully down at the visitor. Partitions

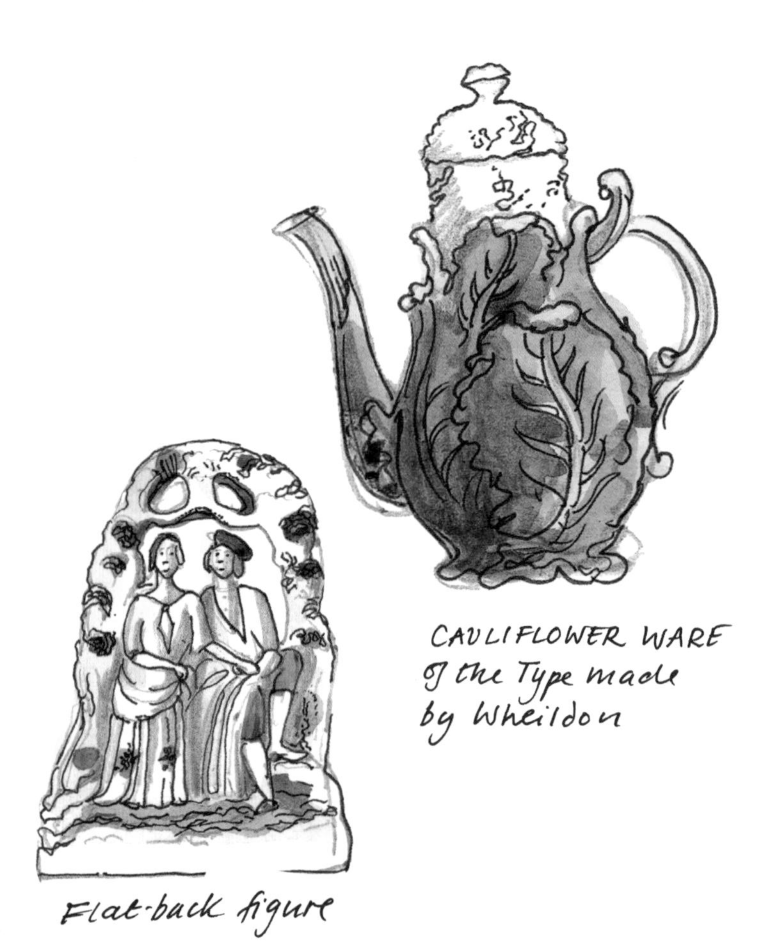

CAULIFLOWER WARE of the Type made by Wheildon

Flat-back figure

divide rooms like police stations in the Ealing comedies and in grimy glazed cabinets are wares commemorative and highly decorated, celebrating the short-lived reign of Edward VIII, the marriage of the Princess Royal to Gerald Lascelles or the inauguration of various trade organizations, the driving forces of which are many years dead and forgotten. Heavy ledgers record transactions between parties now untraceable or dust-choked efforts to right crises of post-war balance sheets or maximize profits from sales to Rhodesia or to Ceylon.

Further into this set of museum-offices is the showroom, like a restrained and low-budget dining room in an interwar ocean liner that has found itself unaccountably landlocked in the grimy valleys of north Staffordshire. The faded bird's-eye maple veneer panelling, jazzy lines of the oval boardroom table and soft fawn leather of the Art Deco chairs still seem poised to accommodate buyers from across the Atlantic or Indian Oceans; and while built to celebrate the centenary of the company in 1951 the showroom is very much a product of the aesthetic of the 1930s.

It is well past bedtime for the original world of Burgess and Leigh. The buyers, their shops and indeed the very countries in which they traded have now gone. Nevertheless the building is not abandoned. Generous grants from English Heritage have kept the roofs on most of it and inside its antique walls a determined enterprise, part museum and part small business, survives, run by some late stockists of the company's wares who, saddened by the news that their much-loved supplier was to close its doors for ever, left their shop and decamped to Stoke to keep the place open. Efforts continue to this day to safeguard it: as I write, the Prince's Regeneration Trust, in association with English Heritage, is involved in another rescue package.

So pretty flowery earthenware is still produced in Middleport. Visitors can tour the factory, climbing unbelievably flimsy staircases drifted deep in clay dust indistinguishable from those recorded in photographs

of 1900. Or they can peer into the mould room, where hundred years of discarded models and plaster moulds for ceramic fancies of the Edwardian years sit stacked on picturesque slatted shelves; and they can see the last remaining copper-plate printing room in the world, where sheets of freshly printed tissue travel along an aerial moving washing line, from which they are unclipped by decorators who fix it to blank teapots, plates and bowls prior to glazing with great, and historical, skill. The factory shop, in which a coal fire straight out of Arnold Bennett glows and crackles, is full of the products of this wonderful place.

WEDGWOOD

Josiah Wedgwood is the acknowledged historic king of Stoke. His factory at Etruria defined the city's first industrial epoch and his house, Etruria Hall, looked down on his creation in austere Georgian restraint. Now it is preserved, in a way, but really it is the saddest place in Stoke. This elegant model block is now dwarfed by a giant hotel, bland of plan and ineptly detailed. Its feeble attempts at emulating its distinguished neighbour are insulting and, more significantly, inappropriate in scale. The giant porte cochère and architecturally illiterate motel styling are a painful contrast. It would have been much better to have built it as a totally separate building, leaving the historically significant Etruria Hall restored and unfettered.

Wedgwood led the world in ceramic manufacture. The entire industry was and is indebted to the factory, not only for technical innovation but for training and in the past for design inspiration as well. The arrival of his beautiful and novel Queen's ware (see page 32) dislodged all other wares from fashionability and galvanized the nascent industry into action. Many had been moving into the development of cream-coloured earthenware, but Josiah had refined and refined and developed and developed his experiments – introducing Cornish clay and stone with more sophisticated shapes and glazes – until he produced something so clearly ahead of the competition that it became widely praised and widely imitated, denting the sales of porcelain even in France and Germany and forcing others to follow his ideas. Meissen, for example, made a glazed porcelain and called the style 'Wedgwoodarbeit'.

Queen Charlotte's acceptance of a tea and coffee service, decorated in green and gold, allowed Wedgwood to style himself 'Potter to Her Majesty'. A commission equally important to his success was the famous Frog service. Named for the amphibian badge in its decorated border, this was destined for La Grenouillière, the gothic-style palace that Empress Catherine the Great of Russia was building as a staging post between St Petersburg and her summer residence in Tsarskoe Selo, called by the Finnish-speaking locals Kekerekeksine because it was surrounded by frog-infested marshes. Sir Josiah caused landscape painters to pack their satchels and record all England's greatest country houses, new and old, to decorate the centres of the 944 pieces of pearly cream earthenware which, after judicious display in his Piccadilly showrooms, were packed in wooden crates for delivery to the Russian court.

The Empress requested that each view painted should be topographically accurate and unrepeated within the entire service. The question of shape and decoration was left entirely to J.W.'s professional opinion. He modelled a new shape for the service, the 'Catherine' shape, even designing some entirely new pieces, and had to find and train extra painters to cope with the task of decoration. Twenty-eight painters are known to have worked on the service. Trial pieces show that Wedgwood contemplated using polychrome enamels, but decided in favour of a muted brown/mulberry-colour enamel – an attempt to simplify the task as far as it could be.

Each plate had a hand-painted intricate border broken by a formally rendered bright green and beautifully black-speckled frog, badge of the house, and in the base of the plate were dozens of beautifully painted views of the great houses and sights of England, taken from the views specially commissioned by Wedgwood or copied from contemporary engravings. In total there were 1,244 views of gardens, ruined abbeys, castles, standing stones, romantic landscapes and manor houses, even views of the Thames and of early industrial sites. All this weighed heavily on Wedgwood and he wrote in 1770 that he 'trembles for the Russian service'.

The marketing value of having both the Queen and the Empress of Russia as customers cannot be overstated. Wedgwood, understanding this, is said to have made only £200 on the Frog service, for an outlay of £3,000, but of course when the complete service was displayed in London before being shipped, London Society could see whose house and lands had been included in the views – immortalized even, since the pieces are on display in the Hermitage museum in St Petersburg. In addition – significantly and rewardingly for Wedgwood – they could order duplicates for themselves.

In 1767 Wedgwood commented in a letter to his friend Thomas Bentley on the success of Queen's ware: 'It is really amazing how rapidly the use of it has spread all most over the whole Globe, & how universally it is liked. – How much of this general use, & estimation, is owing to the mode of its introduction – & how much to its real utility & beauty?' Indeed the first sale bills recorded of English pottery auctions in America mention consignments of Queen's ware as significant components.

The royal connection had more to offer. The demonstration and elevation of the status of Wedgwood's work meant that he could patronize some of the leading artists of his day. He was bold in approaching artists of the undoubted standing of George Stubbs (1724–1806) and John Flaxman Jnr (1755–1856) to produce designs for his products, always aware of the advantages of such cross-brand marketing.

John Flaxman Jnr was born at York, the son of a modeller and plaster cast supplier. From an early age he showed considerable artistic skill; in 1770 he joined the Academy Schools, and he was awarded a silver medal a year later. He began to design bas-reliefs and to model portrait medallions for Wedgwood in 1775. He created in wax all the fine jasperware relief modelling, including that used on Wedgwood's recreation of the Portland Vase. Among the most famous of Flaxman's bas-reliefs for Wedgwood are the *Dancing Hours*, and the renowned *Apotheosis of Homer*. In 1787, accompanied by his wife, he journeyed to Rome, where he lived for seven years. During this time he sent designs to Wedgwood, as well as supervising modellers on behalf of the factory. He returned to England in 1794, and then devoted himself chiefly to monumental sculpture. He became a member of the Royal Academy in 1800, and a member of the Academy of Rome in 1816. He also sculpted the circular monument to Josiah which can be seen in the Church of St Peter Ad Vincula in Stoke.

Stubbs had become interested in painting using enamels from the late 1760s. He had an interest in the

WEDGWOOD PLAQUE · RELIEF by FLAXMAN

sciences and was concerned with the ability of oils and canvas to stand up to ageing. Believing that painting in enamel would produce something far more permanent, he began to experiment with different materials as a base, including copper, wanting something that would stand the high temperatures necessary for the firing of the enamel, and which he could get in large sheets. In 1775 he began to investigate the possibility of a ceramic base, a search that brought him into contact with Thomas Bentley, now Wedgwood's partner.

Wedgwood had already been making quite large-scale pottery tablets. From 1777 he tried making for Stubbs tablets of red earthenware, but these became misshapen and cracked in the kiln if they were more than a couple of feet long. So Wedgwood had the difficult task of developing a ceramic that would survive the firing process even in large pieces.

In a letter to Bentley in 1779 Wedgwood expresses Stubbs's hope that his example of painting in enamel on pottery be followed, and comments to the effect that money could be made from this. Wedgwood – though cautious as to the eventual size of panel possible, telling Bentley not to tell Stubbs anything over 30 inches in length could be produced – is clearly hopeful that such a technical achievement would begin a trend.

The process of painting in enamel was also difficult, though suited to someone as scientific and methodical as Stubbs. Each colour had to be painted and fired separately, since each colour fuses at a different temperature; and the colours that needed higher temperatures had to be fired first, or else the lower-temperature colours would be burned and ruined. So each panel had to be painted, transported and fired many times. Each journey of the precious panel must have been unbelievably nerve-wracking.

The last panels known of were fired in 1783 and 1784, with bad results: of 28 that went into the kiln, 24 were 42 inches long, and only an agonizing 4 of the 42-inch panels survived intact. Wedgwood unsurprisingly decided the endeavour was not commercial. These four were not painted, however, until the 1790s. Either he saved up the panels, prizing them regardless and aware that he would never get any more, or he did not want to continue with something that had not proved commercial.

There is also, of course, Wedgwood's involvement with the abolitionist movement: in 1787 he produced the famous 'Am I Not a Man and a Brother?' medallion in jasperware, modelled by William Hackwood. By 1791 thousands of these medallions had been distributed, including several sent to Benjamin Franklin in America, who wrote back saying:

I am distributing your valuable present of cameos among my friends in whose countenances I have seen such marks of being affected by contemplating the figure of the Suppliant (which is admirably executed) that I am persuaded it may have an effect equal to that of the best written pamphlet in procuring honour to those oppressed people.

There is no doubt that Wedgwood felt very deeply about the issue. He met and corresponded with William Wilberforce, a leader of the movement to abolish the slave trade, who visited him at Etruria Hall; he was a member of one of the committees for the Society for the Abolition of Slavery; he distributed in 1792 a pamphlet called 'An Address to the People of Great Britain on the Propriety of Abstaining from West India Sugar and Rum'. He also helped turn popular opinion against slavery essentially by using fashion. The medallions, like so much else of his ware, became very popular. Ladies wore miniature versions of the medallion in their hair

THESE are SAMPLE colour TABS for COBALT. J.W. Kept DRAWERS of These TESTS in his Search for TECHNICAL INNOVATION

COLOURED WARE TABS

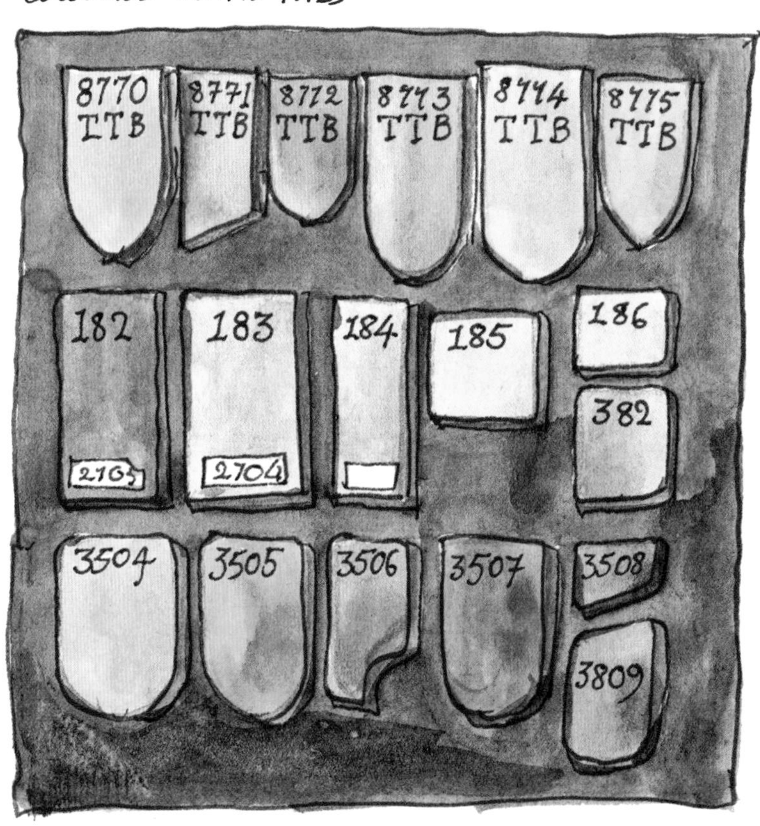

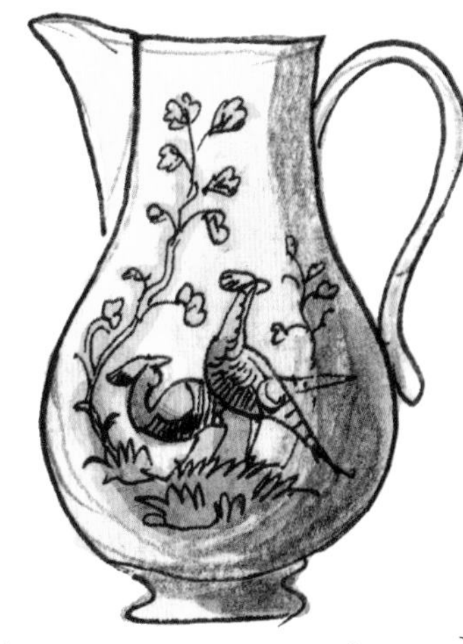

from 1800 when Wedgwood was Austere elegance to...

1850-1900 when it had "Gone Odd"

or in bracelets – a device not unknown today to those opposed to nuclear weapons. While not employed for tea shirts or sports bags, it was used on snuffboxes and hatpins and brooches.

The company's use of innovative artists and designers did not stop with Josiah's death in 1795: it was continued by his successors, who employed Walter Crane (1845–1915) and Eric Ravilious (1903–42), among others.

One of the best-known artists of the 1930s, Eric Ravilious was noted especially for his watercolours and wood engraving. In the Second World War he became an official war artist. He received a commission as a captain in the Royal Marines, and was reported missing at the age of thirty-nine in 1942 when accompanying an air-sea rescue operation off Iceland that did not return to its base. He painted his last pictures as he waited in the North Sea for this fatal mission. He designed a number of stylish and most desirable pottery pieces in the 1930s, which despite the artist's death continued to be produced by the company in the 1950s.

Another artist, this time a native of Staffordshire, who lived in the Villas in Stoke, was Arnold Machin (1911–99). Machin started work at the Minton china factory at the age of fourteen as an apprentice painter and stayed there for seven years before moving to the Crown Derby porcelain works. His association with Wedgwood began in 1940, though in the Second World War he was a conscientious objector and spent twelve months in Wormwood Scrubs. Wedgwood gave him every encouragement: a studio on the new Barlaston estate, extensive facilities for firing his models, special bodies mixed for his use. He worked throughout the 1940s for the company. In 1965 he modelled the Queen's head for the postage stamps – the most reproduced image in the world.

In 2010 this collaboration with external designers continues: designs by Jasper Conran and lesser-known names are still vital yeast leavening the dough of the Wedgwood collection.

Perhaps most significantly Josiah Wedgwood understood the importance of a real connection with his market. Stoke-on-Trent and Staffordshire are, and were, most emphatically not the intended home of his growing industrial output. These wares were for sale in London, Paris and the great new cities of what had recently become the United States of America. Of course he was as much a scientist as a salesman, and the Wedgwood Museum in Barlaston emphasizes this with an exhibit of drawer after drawer of colour, glaze and body stain experiments, testimony to his continuing search for new and more entrancing effects. But the commercial thrust of the business was directed to fulfilling real appetites for pottery in real existing markets.

H.G. Wells had visited the factory fifty years earlier and even then it was considered archaic. He wrote:

. . . considering the great reputation of the firm, I was rather surprised at the ramshackle state of the works, which are, with extension and innumerable patchy alternations, the same that the immortal Josiah erected a century ago; they consist of big, hive-shaped ovens and barn-like but many-storied buildings where the potters and painters work, standing towards each other at all angles, with queer narrow passages and archways penetrating them, with flimsy wooden staircases outside *the building*

and with innumerable windows opaque with dirt and crusted like bottles of ancestral wine with cobwebs and mouldy matter . . .

The factory in 1920 was fast becoming anachronistic, although much loved by its workers, not least because the Wedgwood family were still omnipresent and omnipotent. Not only was Frank Wedgwood (the great-great-grandson of Josiah I) chairman, but among his family also involved in the management were Josiah V (who would succeed as chairman), Tom, Cecil and Hensleigh Wedgwood, not to mention female family members, known to the workforce as 'Miss Joy', 'Miss Star', 'Mrs Frank', etc.

By the 1930s it was apparent that the canalside urban setting of Etruria and its outdated multistorey buildings were no longer the best place to make the huge and successful Wedgwood range. Land was provided in Barlaston, 8 miles south-east of the city and almost within sight of Barlaston Hall, the elegant red brick villa built by the architect Sir Robert Taylor for a lawyer called Thomas Mills in 1756–8 and bought by the Wedgwood family in 1936. Coincidentally, the building had featured on one of the dinner plates of the 1774 Frog service. Some production moved there before the outbreak of the Second World War but the new site did not entirely replace Etruria: it first went into production in 1940, making wares for export and aircraft rivets for the war effort, but the official end of production at Etruria was not until 13 June 1950.

The Barlaston factory was state of the art. Great concrete and steel and asbestos sheds were grouped in this leafy setting with woods alongside and large ex-park trees among the factory buildings. Lorries, like Ladybird book models of prettiness, could drive from end to end of the factory and the very intensive and heavy manual jobs like mould running were gone for ever. Designed by Keith Murray, who was at the time the company's chief designer, and Charles White, it was the first pottery factory in the UK to be entirely electrically fired. This eliminated the risks of breathing in the china-clay dust, which caused silicosis. Its new location also protected the factory from pollution. Impurities, mainly iron from Etruria's neighbour, the Shelton Bar Steel Works, were compromising production, turning the fine white china into flecked 'seconds'. Also, despite Sir Josiah's initial precaution of purchasing mineral rights beneath the Etruria site to a depth of 650 yards, nearby mining and deep seam mining had led to serious subsidence. Indeed the old Etruria factory had by 1930 sunk 8 feet below the canal level.

The site covered 382 acres and the foundation stone was laid on 10 September 1938 with a ceremony in which eight long-serving employees from the Etruria works buried vases and cameos in a casket beneath the foundation stone. Upon it Josiah Wedgwood V placed a plaque that read: 'Within this cavity are buried 8 pots to commemorate the founding of this factory in a Garden Village in the sixth generation of descendants of Josiah Wedgwood who founded his factory at Etruria Staffordshire, 170 years ago. "By their works ye shall know them."' It was not the first such time capsule. The great Burslem potter Enoch Wood had buried just such a hoard beneath the rebuilt Church of St John the Baptist in Burslem in 1828. It contained, among other things, two jugs depicting Lafayette at the Tomb of Franklin; perhaps Wood perceived preserving these to be a particularly powerful political comment.

BLUE AND WHITE

An abandoned cottage is easily lost. Its simple construction, if not of stone, degrades as the weather carries out its war of attrition; as rain, frost and wind take down the roof and shatter the brickwork the ivy-clad hulk is increasingly vulnerable to stormy autumn buffetings. In fifty years or fewer what might once have been the home of a family of eight can become so insubstantial that an afternoon with a digger followed by the plough can wipe it from the next map (although it will remain on the old ones for ever).

Today one man farms where ten did in 1910. Changes in agricultural employment patterns mean that cottages have become genuinely redundant. While the post-war property boom has left many of these lavishly restored, as many others have – for reasons of relative isolation or their position in woods or fields whose owner would prefer them undisturbed – disappeared into the trees or beneath the corduroy of plough.

The cottage's site is now unmarked except for an apple or plum tree in the hedge or a clump of gooseberry bushes in the corner of a field. Even the track that led to it, bound by two unruly hedges of thorn, bramble and elder that provided fruit for the jam, sloe gin or cordials that marked the seasons and a fluffy verge whose cow parsley and milk thistle were repeatedly picked for the immobile rabbit in the hutch and her remote descendants, has gone. Its destruction was only another day's work with JCB and bonfire. The scruffy surface of the track with its changing map of potholes and channels and grass was no more permanent, the walk to school or church that marked the weeks and years wiped out one unsmiling November Monday morning by the powerful mechanized team.

Stay with me. This herring is less luridly red than it might seem, because what is left comes from Stoke. The eager eight-year-old archaeologist and her brother with beach spade and plastic bucket, whose annual pleasure on seeing that field ploughed up again is to scour the cottage site for its second crop, shards of china, are at work. And yet again the bucket is brought back to curatorial headquarters with a harvest of domestic earthenware, evidence of life in that field corner. Those cups and saucers, plates and dishes, shattered into stamp-sized pieces, are the story not only of the cottage kitchen but of the everyday output of distant Stoke, because though tis cottage is in Norfolk it might equally be in Devon or Cornwall,

These SHARDS were all found on a BUILDING site in HANLEY in 2010.

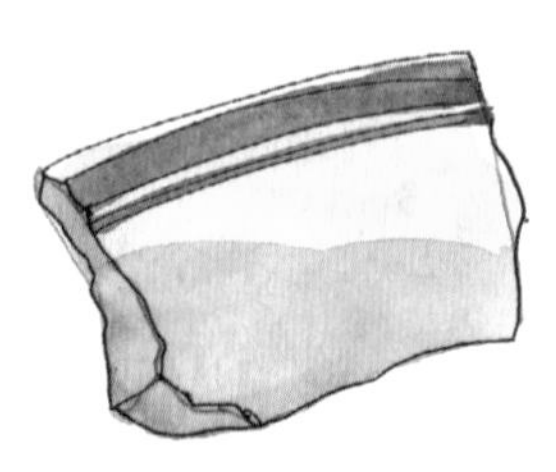

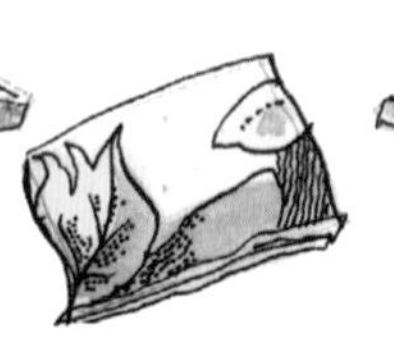
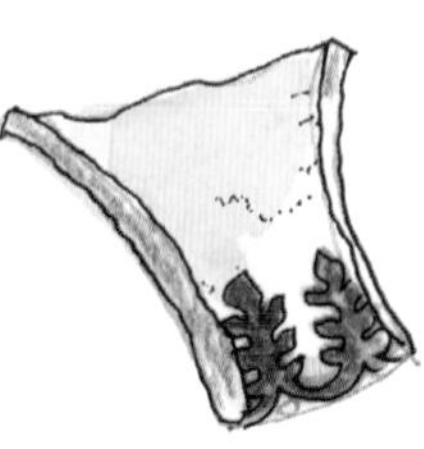

Kent or Sussex, Powys or Cardiganshire, or indeed Tierra del Fuego. Reduced to cockle-shell-sized fragments, some pieces may be hard to visualize in their entirety and impossible to identify, but what will appear every time is **blue and white**.

These fragments with a lion's head, a tree trunk, a girl on a swing or perhaps part of an oriental bridge are engraved ware. The technique of engraving, so quintessentially, recognizably the product of the Staffordshire potteries, was in fact developed by John Sadler and Guy Green , tilemakers in 1756 in Liverpool and was revolutionary. The image was engraved on to a copper plate from which a tissue-paper impression was taken and applied to a tile. This was glazed and fired, during which process the paper was burnt away, leaving only the ceramic colour as printed on the face of the tile.

Being so obviously an advance with applications beyond the world of tile manufacture, the technique quickly attracted the attention of that visionary innovator Josiah Wedgwood and unsurprisingly a partnership with Sadler and Green was established in 1761. This opened the floodgates of cheaper decoration and Wedgwood's modish creamware proved the ideal substrate for this new technology, initially with Liverpool tradesmen John Sadler and Guy Green producing the printed paper components.

Stoke being a city given to inventiveness, it was not long before these 'transfers' were being produced in the city itself and a new ancillary industry was established along the banks of the canal. The upheavals of the French Revolution delivered M. Foudriner via Dartford to Hanley and, in 1806, he set up a tissue-paper mill on the banks of the Caldon canal; and various printers were in business by the end of the decade.

The engraved technique, either in black or more usually in various strengths of cobalt blue, quickly became a mainstay of the city's output. Most notable among those to utilize the new technique was Spode, in particular its Blue Italian pattern. With variations of great significance to the devotee but barely visible to the user, the jugs and bowls, plates and dishes in blue and white were produced continuously until the middle of the nineteenth century, when a muddled desire for elaboration caused the fashion to move on to more gilded fripperies. However, production continued and indeed continues today both at Portmeirion and in the crumbling factory of Burgess and Leigh at Middleport.

As blue and white engravings were more a decorative language than a single design idea, the variation of subject matter is quite extraordinary, as indeed is the choice of shapes, that choice of course being all the shapes. But certain themes recur: rural scenes, frequently with animals in a leading role; Aesop's fables and scenes from antiquity and mythology; sporting scenes and specific buildings, for example

They represent the varied production of the CITY in about 1900.

Windsor Castle, both appropriate for the increasingly well-travelled Englishman who made use of the new communications networks that were being established at the time, and also for an increasingly established nationalism. The expansion of the Empire gave rise to a plethora of international – particularly Indian – designs, both for export and for home consumption. Other themes covered included clubs and organizations, buildings and industrial successes, and, of course, military events. In fact, what this cheap and adaptable method of decoration had become was a means of communication, a way of promoting political causes, such as the Reform Bill, or of celebrating a hero – the Duke of Wellington perhaps or Lord Nelson – or the erection of a new station, bridge or factory. Although the costs of engraving were considerable, they were not so great as to preclude the printing of a short run for a special event; indeed had the custom remained current for longer there would have been 'Sinking the *Belgrano*' jugs and 'Fall of Berlin Wall' meat plates available at the appropriate moment.

Technologies spawn art forms. The wide-spanned and well-lit ceilings of Renaissance Italy cried out for the frescoes of Michelangelo, Tintoretto or Veronese. The current digital revolution has created a whole world of computer graphics and game design. Similarly architects and designers flocked to work on schemes for cars or ocean liners when they were new. In the same way the engraved decoration of earthenware was freely adopted by the burgeoning middle-class society of late eighteenth- and nineteenth-century England to which it was so perfectly suited.

Like a lot of eighteenth-century ceramics the blue and white craze was founded on a desire to emulate the wares shipped from China. The nascent European ceramic industry looked enviously at the pearly white decorated porcelain that formed the cargoes clipping through the China Seas and around the Cape of Good Hope to Bristol or London – as seen in those cargoes of this valuable commodity that have been dragged from wrecks to the seas' surface, in the same condition that they left the warehouses in Shanghai or Canton (a good instance of the durability of ceramics). All across Europe these glossy wares – plates and jugs, vases and bowls, often decorated with armorial devices carefully copied in the workshops of the East – were the ceramic background to refined life. You see them in Dutch still lifes and in Hogarth's engravings of the interiors of Georgian London.

The Josiahs, Woods, Weildens and Adams resented the wasted opportunity that these imports represented and, as we have seen, strived continuously to produce a whiter ware that would oust the China trade and gain that business for Staffordshire. Through repeated trials and experiments, comparable cream and white wares were discovered and these did, in due course, reduce the oriental imports to a trickle. But a lingering appetite for the aesthetic of the East survived. Those decorative elements, so long considered the acme of sophisticated and metropolitan tastes, survived and resurfaced in home-produced wares in the oriental style, and nowhere is this more pronounced than in the **Willow pattern** design.

There are certain patterns in pottery that claim recognition beyond the circle of the obsessive collector. Napoleon Ivy, that restrained and elegant Regency scheme allegedly conceived by Wedgwood as decoration for the plates containing the gloomy soups and stews enjoyed by the lately great and by then much reduced Emperor of France in exile on the Island of Elbe, continued to be produced for over a hundred years. Royal Albert Roses, the definitive tasteless granny pattern, is apparently still bought for, or even by, grannies of the generation who attended the Festival of Britain and believed design could change the world, and will no doubt be equally popular amongst those grannies who rolled bare breasted and daisy painted on the flattened grass of Knebworth.

But no pattern can hold a candle to that utter pot-boiling/cross-dresser/all-time-golden-oldie the Willow pattern. Generations of schoolchildren have, with varying degrees of ineptitude, copied the image whose elements –

Two birds flying high
A Chinese vessel sailing by.
A bridge with three men, sometimes four,
A willow tree, hanging o'er.
A Chinese temple, there it stands,
Built upon the river sands
An apple tree, with apples on,
A crooked face to end my song

– are so easily digested and whose story, surely an amalgam of a hundred post-rationalizing explanations, has been told by Miss for a hundred years. The pattern has been drawn artlessly on to a million paper plates to be proudly taken home and displayed alongside an example of the real thing hastily unearthed from some kitchen cupboard. Current deskilling in the classroom has in some cases reduced such efforts to colouring in a photocopied rendering of the design, thus utterly losing sight of the fact that Willow pattern is blue and white china and represents, through the medium of transfer printing, a direct channel back to the tastes of seventeenth- and eighteenth-century London.

Later developments in engraving, initially at the Spode factory, led to a new method of delivery, where the design was printed not on to fine tissue paper but on to a silicone bombe, from which it was transferred by direct printing on to the biscuit surface of the plate. This device, the Murray Curvex machine (enshrining the name of its inventor), and the use of the plastic-coated transfer have now supplanted the copper-plate and tissue-paper method in all but two establishments, one of which, Burgess and Leigh, still maintains the whole scheme of presses and plates and a strange half railway/half washing-line system that delivers the freshly printed sheets of tissue around the workshop – an extraordinary sight.

But today the taste for blue and white engraving is much diminished and the province of the collector, not of the high-street shopper.

This DISTINGUISHED Blue and White Coffee Pot was made c 1800

TILES

Tiles are quite another thing. Tile making is a well-established industry today. H. & E. Heath makes the tiled walls for London's Underground. One of the city's giants is Johnson Tiles, which is hugely mechanized and produces a million tiles a month. Among its many claims to fame is a mountain of fired ceramic waste. This heap is the final resting place for a lot of shraff, the cracked, blistered, misshaped or discoloured chuck-outs of many of Stoke's factories. This shorthand exhibition of the city's output in fragmented form is massive. But it is not a sinister symbol of mankind's wastefulness and the looming cloud of destruction hanging over us. Rather it is a bit of good news, for it will reappear, phoenix-like, as new tiles. The mix required for the company's tiles includes 25–38 per cent of fired waste and these shards, previously used to fill marl pits or as foundation material, are now a useful component.

Tiles have been produced in England for centuries. The floors of our medieval churches were composed, or partially composed, of encaustic tiles. These durable hand-made floor tiles were decorated with patterns of contrasting coloured clays, which were then glazed and fired. Hundreds of thousands of these survive in subtle combinations of earthy colours, some with striking tonal contrasts. The most basic are purely geometric. Those in the church at Helpstone in Northamptonshire, for example, are in a pattern of tiny tessellating tiles forming slim lozenges, radiating circles and combinations of the two. Others depict animals or, that mainstay of the medieval subconscious, mounted gentlemen in pursuit of those animals. Others still are decorated with symbols religious or secular, crosses, crowns or orbs. Later in the fourteenth and fifteenth centuries complex armorial designs and other elaborate compositions were constructed of these inlaid clays.

A circumcontinental drift of new technologies and skills began in China and travelled in the first millennium, padding on camel toes along the ancient Silk Route across the desert of Central Asia to settle and develop in Turkey and Persia before moving westwards again with the scimitar-wielding Muslim conquerors of Spain and Portugal.

Here the mysteries of the tile maker were to flourish and take root; indeed the façades of countless townhouses, churches, cloisters and other public buildings throughout the Iberian peninsula are today still covered from pavement to eaves in boldly patterned ceramic tiles. But the early tile makers were Moors and it was their Islamic style, with cursive text and floral motifs on blue cobalt and green copper oxide tiles, that covered the patios of Grenada and Cordoba.

Developments and dynastic mergers of the medieval and Renaissance ages disseminated these skills first to Italy and then, most significantly, to the Netherlands. In the mid–seventeenth century, when Vermeer was painting his calm orderly interiors, *The Girl with a Pearl Earring* et al, no room – or at any rate no fireplace or stove – was complete without its surround of blue and white Delft tiles. It was the taste for these, no doubt developed nationally during the exile of the House of Stuart during the protectorate of Oliver Cromwell, that brought the tile and the tilewright back to Britain. The craft was concentrated in London and, to a lesser extent, in the ports of Bristol and Liverpool. Less than a century later the tile-making industry was established in Stoke-on-Trent.

Josiah Wedgwood, unsurprisingly, was at the forefront of developments and his dealings with the engravers of

Liverpool, described on page 49, no doubt spurred him on to develop his own tile business. But it was the tile works of Minton in the 1930s that both developed the trade into a fine art and decorated the porches and halls of not only Stoke-on-Trent but also Britain and its dependencies.

The Minton tile was a cultural phenomenon at the heart of the British Empire; indeed it might, by the more bitter observer, be seen as a tool of imperialism and class distinction. The floors of the villas in Stoke, for example, were entirely of Minton tiles, but those at the front of the house, in the parlour, hall, study, conservatory and dining room, were of complex and beautiful design, while those at the rear, the preserve of the domestic staff, were of plain terracotta or black and devoid of decoration. However, those with less of an axe to grind would notice that many of the plain terraced houses of Stoke-on-Trent sport jolly panels on either side of a porch or on the floor. Once established, the use of tiles as architectural ornament became almost standard.

The modest works of A. Wood, Tiles, Cement on Regent Road has just such a scheme. The unexceptional building of stock brick with minimal decoration is transformed by three panels trumpeting the business's name in stoneware letters. This is just the sort of building that, though unlisted, continues to characterize the whole nature of Stoke. Its loss would be grave. The bricks-and-mortar narrative continues across the road, where an unexceptional late nineteenth-century house, in a terrace, is distinguished from its neighbours by an elaborate moulded porch. A complex gothic hood mould is supported by hefty square stops. They need to be substantial to bear the monogram ARW, the initials of Ambrose Wood, whose manufactory sits opposite, a complete illustration of the history of Stoke in brick tile.

Herbert Minton's great partnership with the first high priest of the Gothic Revival Augustus Pugin began in the late 1830s. The two collaborated on the church of St Giles, Cheadle, where the latter's desire to reinstate the techniques of medieval encaustic tiles was married to the ingenuity of Minton's technical mind, giving rise to a polychrome explosion of astonishing force (see page 83).

TRANSFER DECORATED TILE in the ARTISTIC or AESTHETIC

STYLE. made © 1880

Artists of the Aesthetic and Queen Anne Revival movement, like Walter Crane and Kate Greenaway, produced countless designs on which the Minton company, by then Minton Hollins, collaborated. The fireplaces of the greenery-yallery artistic folk of Kensington and their lesser followers throughout the new suburbs of London, Manchester, Glasgow or any other major city were lined, or at the very least edged, with tiles decorated with skilfully drawn flora and fauna. Then came the bulb-bursting, frond-thrusting wildness of the Art Nouveau, a school of design based not on its particular newness, although it was a distinct departure from the historicism of the mid- and late Victorian era, but on its drawing its inspiration directly from nature itself. It is an irony that this style, so keen to dissociate itself from any previous period, should be so firmly stuck in its own, for the sinuous vines and curvilinear foliage that cover the Paris Metro are firmly rooted in the *fin de siècle* earth.

While architectural ceramics and the fascias and balustrades of a thousand or ten thousand pubs, billiard halls or temperance clubs were as likely to be made in Doulton's London factory, established in 1815, the tiles would most likely come from Stoke.

STOKE IN THE 1950s

This is an account of what it was like designing for the ceramic industry in the early 1950s. Pat Albeck was a young designer, born in 1930. For her, fresh out of art school, the grimy and industrially active cities of the north were the place where her designs would be realized, and thus they were imbued with a curious glamour. They still have that appeal to her today when she visits, although Stoke is now the only city that is still producing what it was fifty years ago.

I was lucky to have started my career when the manufacturing industry was healthy and prosperous. Cities like Manchester, Stoke-on-Trent, Sheffield and Belfast were all flourishing.

In the second year of my textile course at the Royal College of Art, Bobby Baker, who ran the school of ceramics, was called upon to run the textile school. He was well known in the Potteries (he had been principal of Burslem Art School) and had close connections with all the fine china companies. He liked my designs and thought I might try adapting my work for pottery decoration. Many ceramic departments at art schools at that time were concentrating on studio pottery, studying shape and form, with a minimum of decoration, so a textile designer, with a background of drawing and painting, particularly flowers, which I did, was useful. Pottery manufacturers needed decoration: they had been starved of new patterns for a long time. Bobby Baker showed my work to some of the fine china manufacturers, and as they seemed interested I found myself going to Stoke-on-Trent as well as Manchester.

My pottery designs were very different from those for cloth. They were much more considered, careful and restrained. The finished product was more expensive to produce: it cost more to buy and it had to last longer. Buying a dinner service was different from buying a cotton dress, which lasted a short time. Fashion came out seasonally, but a dinner or tea service was introduced with care; it might have to last a lifetime. If the design was a success, it became a standard pattern, which meant you could go on for some time buying replacements. The dinner service was expensive, not a casual purchase, and more often than not it would be bought as a major wedding present. Brides would be asked the date and place of the wedding, followed by 'Have you chosen your dinner service?'

This was before the arrival of the cheerful mug. Designs for mugs, after all, can change as quickly as fashion fabrics.

I have always liked designing on paper and then seeing the design through to the finished product, enjoying the process of carefully matching the colours and overseeing the interpretation on to the finished product. I was used to visualizing my work on cloth, and translating my patterns on to three-dimensional products was very different. Pottery production was new to me, so I had to visit the Potteries a few times. Designing for china was a serious matter.

Early morning travel involved breakfast. London Midland always provided excellent breakfasts (with kippers, if you liked). I would enjoy every moment of the journey to Stoke-on Trent, the train rushing north until you reached the station with the magic name of Etruria. (I never left the train here, since I never worked for Wedgwood.) Then the sight of the wonderfully shaped kilns, in red brick, with huge clouds of black smoke belting out – the sign that told me I was approaching Stoke. Clutching my folder of designs, I would step into the station, a very impressive mid-Victorian building, the interior of red brick and glazed tiles. The façade is much the same today.

The visit would be very formal. It was a design meeting, to be taken seriously; nothing but the best would do. I was always met by the owner of the firm or the managing director. He would certainly be wearing a well-cut tweed jacket and sober tie. I myself would not dream of going to a design meeting without wearing gloves. Stepping into Winton Street, with the North Staffordshire Hotel across the road, there would be a rather large car, in which I was taken to the factory. If I was visiting Spode I would be met by one of the Mr Copelands, the owners. That was very impressive.

The buildings, I seem to remember, were all made of quite a dark red brick. When I arrived at around 9.00 a.m. everyone would already be at work, but the streets were still busy enough with shoppers and lots of trams. There were no huge hoardings selling fast food; there may have been a film poster advertising the programme at a tile-faced but grimy Art Deco cinema. But apart from normal terraced houses and shops, every building seemed to be devoted to the making of pots. We would pass countless factories, some of them actual potteries with a familiar pottery manufacturer's name in tile patterns or ironwork.

The names of the potteries are so nostalgic and were really special to me. Pottery manufacturers' names, rather like French couturiers', were rather purred over. Spode, Minton, Dior, Givenchy . . . One might have seen them together on shop fronts in Bond Street in London, but here in Stoke was where the magic product was made. These were not museum shops but real factories actually making things.

There were certain unspoken rules about the design of tableware at this time. The customer, particularly in the American market, and especially the American bride, had to have a white centre or base to their plate. The pattern had to be only on the border; the food to be eaten could have no pattern underneath it. If you were very bold you could have a little leaf coming over the border on to the well. Of course the designer always wants to break rules, and I did from time to time. Colour was quite muted, even on the border. There was a preponderance of pale greyish greens and blues.

The factories I visited all had decorative and impressive entrances. Inside, there were thick carpets and glass showcases with examples of important pieces from the past or samples of current ranges.

I would be taken to the boardroom to show my work to other directors. It is always a bit of a worry showing designs; they may have looked impressive at home, but showing them to important people in the industry is another matter. What a relief it was when they liked them, and then called in the design director, in a spotless white coat. If they decided to go ahead with a design, the work then started. We would discuss methods of printing and what was the most suitable shape for the pattern. The pattern was always sampled on a dinner plate. If it was successful, I would then design the actual fittings, the way the design fits the plate or cup, for other pieces that we had decided to produce. Methods of production were not much more difficult before the arrival of the computer; they just took a lot longer.

Design discussions over, we would approach the important matter of lunch. The Spode factory had a directors' dining room and employed a cook for the directors. I hope the workforce had something half as nice, for I remember the trifle fifty-eight years later. I made such a fuss about that trifle that the cook always made it when she knew I was coming.

Next door to the dining room was a small, very exciting museum, a wonderful collection of historic examples of the company's ware. There were some wonderful pieces of early Blue and Red Tower, and my favourite Blue Gloucester, huge serving dishes, commemorative dinner services and modelled pieces. I was taken to see the Trent and Mersey canal just behind the factory and the smaller canals leading to it. Carrying pottery by boat was safer than other methods of transport, and in the 1950s the canals were still used to transport clay to the factory, and to take finished ware for packaging and delivery. After a tour of the factory I would be taken back to the station, with instructions about further work.

Albeck's experience of the city does appear to be very culinary and as she is my mother and still telephones me to say what she is cooking for lunch I do not find this at all surprising. Most, if not all, of the dining rooms are gone. I bought the Copeland Spode dining-room chairs as a job lot when the factory was being stripped of all its contents in September 2009. Today designs are more likely to arrive at the remaining Stoke potteries from the south via email. Art students and young designers still struggle with outsize portfolios as they arrive off the absurdly expensive Virgin west coast line train. They are likely to be hoping to get a place at the very good surface pattern or ceramic courses at the art school, currently trading as the University of Staffordshire. They come from all over the country but never wear the neat little gloves that even I remember my mother sending hundreds of miles to Pullers of Perth to be cleaned.

WHAT HAPPENED TO THE POTTERIES

Another fantasy
Mr Paul walks past the last three houses of Benet Street with his head down. Adele watches him from her bedroom window, setting her clock by his arrival at the potbank at which all her family work. Andrew, a caster, is now helped by young Will and all three girls as decorators. Her father, in dead-brown cotton coat, has managed the warehouse for fifteen years and his younger brother, also Adele's next-door neighbour, has spent ten years carefully marking the barrels of ware with the name of the country to which it will be shipped.

In the factory Uncle Paul straightens his thin tie, sniffs the shellac in the ink in which his stubby stencilling brush is sitting and takes down a galvanized plate of tin, out of which the world 'CEYLON' is cut, holds it tight against the chestnut lathe of a barrel and dabs on the doomed word. Six dozen lustrous cobalt-blue cups and saucers are ready to load on to the canal.

But when they reach Liverpool they are actually part of the last shipment to be checked by Major Harvey, who has recently taken this civilian job, as his Indian Army regiment has been disbanded. The Harveys have worked and lived in the greatest of HM's dominions for five generations. If Adele was equally genealogically aware this timespan would coincide exactly with her own family's life in the potteries. Her great-great-grandfather Joseph, surname unknown both to her and to the gangmaster for whom he worked, was a 'Paddy', a farmless farmer from County Clare, who came to dig the grand trunk canal in 1770.

The industrial machine of Stoke – indeed of all of Britain – is inextricably bound up with Empire and Adele is right to worry as she watches Mr Paul with her nervous smile as he looks up at the house on his way home. All is not well and orders are crumbling; the three branches of E. Impey Ltd (general dealers) of Madras, Calcutta and Simla are not the only good customers whose sad letter has confirmed that their door has closed once and for all. From Rangoon to Ootamacund the businesses have folded and as

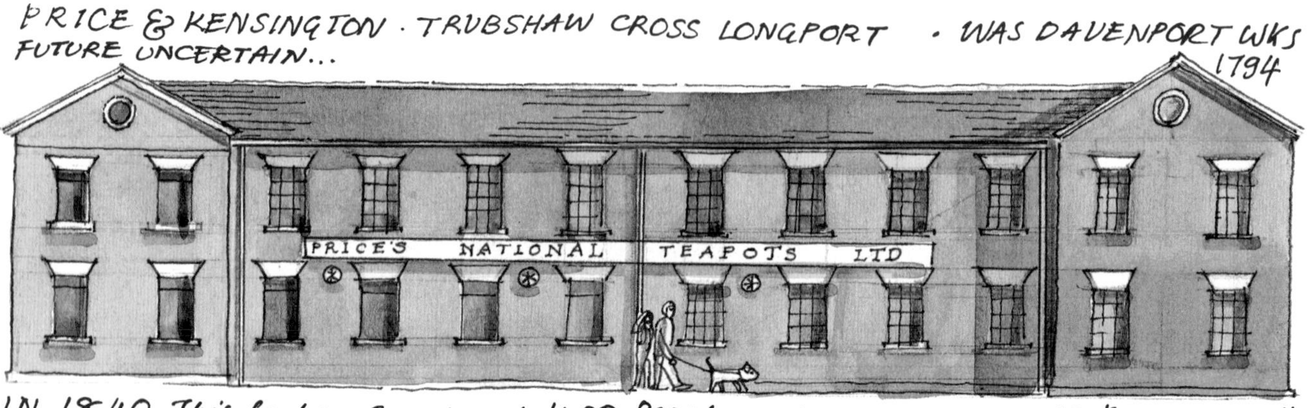

the Imperial possessions are lost so is the ready market for ordinary ceramic goods, the bread and butter of Stoke's output.

Adele is old, so old; she is ninety-two. None of her family now works on the potbank, although thirty or forty people still do and she still watches them leave, no horn or bell now. She narrows her eyes at Miss Choudry, the only connection now with the subcontinent, who without asking passes her ten Rothmans and a box of Swan Vestas before slipping noiselessly behind the PO counter to hand out the last pension payment Adele will collect.

Now these fictitious characters and the real workers they represent are all dead. Their lives are linked to the city, however. They are Stoke, as are the Hungarians who fled here in 1956, the Italians and the newcomers, or the Tajiks, only passing through the city, who wash your car in Lichfield Street and dream of a cold clear-blue sky and eagles soaring on the thermals or nodding oil wells gushing money.

The Potteries no longer equip the tables of the Empire; in fact the jobs have been exported instead. Factories in China and India are sending their cheap export ware here: Stoke is now the consumer.

Employment in the pottery industry in Stoke was at its peak in 1925, when it employed 100,000 people, its annual output was £2 billion and the plates, cups and saucers, teapots and trinkets that made up that figure travelled the world. In 1948 80,000 were employed in pottery in Stoke-on-Trent, in 1958 70,000 (when 94 per cent of pottery workers in the UK were concentrated in this small area of north Staffordshire), in 1968 62,000, in 1991 22,500. In 2000–2001 there were still about 20,000 employed in pottery and another 20,000 in ancillary industries: colour and glaze producers, machinery suppliers. In 2009 (according to a report in which the sector is rather unpoetically called 'non-metallic minerals'), the pottery industry accounted for only 4 per cent of employment in north Staffordshire, although 25 per cent of manufacturing jobs – in real figures that is approximately 6,000 jobs plus an estimated 3,000 in the ancillary industries.

In 1958 there were 2,000 bottle kilns in use. Today there are 47 bottle kilns and all cold as the grave. In 1958, there were 298 pottery factories, 438 of the bottle kilns still in use, and 654 tunnel/other gas and electric kilns in use.

People have not abandoned the plate, but many have abandoned the place. The discrepancy between English and Portuguese wages in the 1980s was already telling. Peter got £2.35 per hour, Pedro £1.03. Unsurprisingly companies began to 'outsource'. That between England and China in the 1990s was greater still. Charlie's pay

DOULTON & CO MOVED to The NILE St WORKS of PINDER, BOURNE & CO in 1882. In 1901 They acquired the Royal WARRANT, becoming ROYAL DOULTON. Most of the factory is now demolished. The remainder lies empty...

"I have been employed for about six years. I get PLAY DAYS at Easter Christmas, Whitsun and Wakes & Races." Thomas Massey aged 13.

was up – hooray! – to £3.50, but Chan's was a factory-moving £0.30. Oh dear! Manufacturers were tempted further still, and as Malaysia and Indonesia also proved eager to enter the global low wages market the imperative to chase profits became all-powerful, particularly for businesses that were anyway only parts of large industrial groups with large and varied share ownership. (In 1799 the import duty on Chinese porcelain was 108 per cent – a persuasive encouragement to people to buy domestically made china. What effect would an imposition of this sort of tariff have on the industry today? All international trade agreements would, of course, preclude such a plan, but it would at a stroke remove the greater part of the price advantage an increasingly expensive Chinese production system has over our own.)

Spode moved 80 per cent of its manufacturing to Indonesia; Doulton 75 per cent of its capacity first to Malaysia and then to Indonesia. Portmeirion, founded in Stoke by Susan Williams-Ellis and her husband Euan Cooper-Willis in 1960, began to produce in Portugal. Most surprisingly of all, the flagship of the fleet quietly changed its colours and sailed under a flag of convenience, losing 80 per cent of its workforce as the world-famous designs of Sir Josiah Wedgwood's company began to be turned out by the now highly skilled workforces of South East Asia, trained by technicians sent out from Stoke by the directors of Wedgwood and Doulton.

Outsourcing was not the only change. Mechanization has also played a part, and perhaps that news is good. Some jobs may have gone but Dudson, off whose plates hundreds of thousands of Little Chef visitors wolf their hash browns each morning, employed 300 in 1960 and employ 300 today, and their output has gone up by 300 per cent. Similar increases have been achieved at other hotelware companies, Steelite and Churchill. Stoke-on-Trent still makes catering china for the world.

Where are the still-famous brands described as working in the city in 1954 in British Potters and Pottery today – among them Adams, Alcock, Beswick, Cauldon Crown Staffordshire, Price Kensington, Hammersley, Grindley, Sadlers, Mason's, Ridgeway, New Hall and Minton? (The list of all the potteries appears on page 148, along with similar records of those in production in 1802, 1787 and 1715. Some names – Wedgwood, Adams and Wood – feature in all lists.)

For the old names of English ceramics, things are a little shaky. Wedgwood survives, but in 1999 the company went into administration. Shortly afterwards I walked round its Barlaston factory to look at some kilns.

The kilns are up for grabs – in fact almost everything there is up for grabs. The workers – there are currently about 400. There may be further rationalization, a focusing on the manufacture of premium wares and a consolidation into one or two buildings. All other manufacture will be continued in Indonesia. Meanwhile even to stop and look at a machine is uneasy-making, perhaps indicative to its operator of his being one of the unlucky ones. These are not people whose children will want to go into the ceramics industry, on to the potbanks. Indeed if they lose their own jobs they are unlikely to return to pottery. However, this being Stoke-on-Trent, the workforce is smiling and unreasonably friendly and chatty, including the overseer of the robotic cup-making plant.

This is a completely extraordinary thing. In a glass box the size of a bus stop is a cream-painted steel plinth; from it rise two rather sinister limbs, on the end of which emerge hands rather like Black & Decker drills with three fingers. In the middle is a turntable with a series of discs in the manner of a merry-go-round. At peace this is dull and lifeless, but when the room comes to life these arms take on a supernatural and utterly compelling personality for, with compressed air and vacuum, hydraulics and bearings and all the attendant tricks of the engineer's mystery, the robot within picks up each cup with infinite grace and loveliness, its totally independent other arm takes a handle between its steel talons and with the refinement of Audrey Hepburn carefully and unfailingly fits handle to cup. This done, the cup is carefully laid to rest on a rack, shortly to be shepherded to the great tunnel kilns not by a white-coated operative but by a Mini-Cooper-sized orange truck with all-seeing invisible eyes forever chirruping and bleeping its presence. In fact she is not all benign: she has recently pinned a worker relentlessly against the factory wall until rescued by a distant fellow.

It is impossible not to see the robot as enchanting and to be impressed by the quarter of a million cups a week she can make – or is it a day? But do Wedgwood need them? The machine is designed to run twenty-four hours a day, seven days a week, but that is not happening and the neighbouring pair of arms are inert in their box. As we pass by, a machinery dealer in our group says, '250,000 cups a week. Trouble was sales and marketing weren't keeping up with it.' Perhaps that defines the upside-down nature of the problem. We live in a post-dinner-service age and the robot has not been informed. A machine, or indeed any other way of manufacturing, cannot dictate business. Businesses need to find out what their customers want to buy and then make it in whatever way they find best. Advertising and other forms of marketing can suggest and endeavour to influence the customers' choice, but they can't, and surely shouldn't, bully those customers.

But people can be reskilled: they can be trained to do quite another job. In fact, it was traditional in Stoke to be uneasy about a factory with sparkly white new-painted walls: they were seen as an indication of insolvency, as they had no doubt been decorated by factory hands for whom there was no other work. As I left the factory I told the robot's minder that I thought his charge was beautiful to watch. 'Yes,' he said, 'but you can't chat her up, can you?'

Misunderstanding his market is a trap into which Josiah Wedgwood successfully avoided. But perhaps one of the main cracks in Stoke-on-Trent today is that consumers have become more sophisticated and that anyway they are not in dire need of very much in the way of household goods. Sixteenth- and seventeenth-century wills are very specific in their itemization of bequests. Spoons, sheets, beds and plate are listed and directed to their new owner, alongside land and other property. For example, here is the will of Thomas Herries (who might have seen a play by W. Shakespeare on stage):

A true and perfect inventorye of all and singuler the goods and chattells of Thomas Herries late deceased in the parishe of St. Gregoryes in Norwich prysed by us William Rogers and Gregorye Wesbye the xvth daye of October in the year of our Lord God 1599.

In primis:	one borded bedsted	3s. 4d.
Item:	one mattresse and one under cloathe	1s. 6d.
Item:	one flocke bed	2s. 6d.
Item:	one bolster	2s. 0d.
Item:	one downe pillowe and an old cushaigne	1s. 6d.
Item:	two leather pillows filled with feathers	3s. 4d.
Item:	one payer of sheets	2s. 0d.
Item:	one drye barrel	3d.
Item:	one old cofer	2s. 0d.
Item:	2 salt boxes	1s. 0d.
Item:	one hake, a fryer pann, a payer of tonges and a rostinge yron	1s. 6d.
Item:	one litle ketle, a sawer and 3 pewter spoones	2s. 6d.
Item:	3 little boles	1s. 0d.
Item:	One ketle, one potspone, 28 trenyens	1s. 0d.
Item:	2 woodinge platters and 5 dishes and twoo erthen potts	8d.
Item:	a stone pott and 5 galley pottes	4d.
Item:	a hamper and certen old washe	6d.
Item:	4 frayles and 2 stooles	6d.
Item:	a little table and 4 stoles	3s. 0d.
Item:	3 chiselles, 2 hamers and a perser	8d.
Item:	3 old cushings	6d.
Item:	2 payers of hand cuffes and one dozen of hand kerchers and an old pillowbere	2s. 6d.
Item:	2 old shirtes	1s. 8d.
Item:	One old forme and 2 old cappes	1s. 0d.
Total:		£1 18s. 5d.

Mr Herries was a labourer (so he would have watched the play on his feet). His inventory is an indication of the rarity of domestic effects in an earlier age. In a later, American, will of 1780, John Carlyle's pottery is listed after the furniture and linen, before the slaves and farm implements, and includes '5 Queens China dishes defferent Scize', valued at £2.0.0. The will contains over forty other lots of pottery, some containing as many as twenty pieces. Contrast this with the belongings of Thomas Herries and his two 'erthen potts'. What the two have in common is that their household goods were deemed worthy of record, and indeed of passing on.

Now, when the manufacture and ownership of household items increased dramatically, their rarity has faded and their perceived value diminished. The kudos attached to the possession of a dinner service is much reduced. The barrels of plates that travelled out to the new American West on the paddle steamer in Oklahoma in the early nineteenth century contained status symbols; but today, when our material riches are so much greater, a shiny new dinner set is no more the defining symbol of success than is a piano, the most expensive item in so many Victorian parlour.

However, despite our own effects being of such little value as to make an inventory of our bowles and turreenes laughable, today Wedgwood is not moribund. Sales are, confusingly, quite strong, its turnover high. Most – 80 per cent – of its manufacture is still sourced abroad, principally in Indonesia; it crosses the South China Seas and makes the journey from Liverpool to Stoke for dispatch in a sad contrast to Sir Josiah's barge trips in the opposite direction. The factory may be slimmed down to anorexic proportions, but smart platinum-striped Jasper Conran Wedgwood cups and saucers will still emerge from the kilns at Barlaston, along with other 'premium' products.

Last week I stayed, in the Upper House Hotel in Barlaston (see page 86). At breakfast I talked to two neat and achingly fashionable Japanese ladies in their twenties. They had come to visit Wedgwood. They did not know there were any other potteries in Stoke and were travelling on to London, two days, Oxford, one, and the Cotswolds before leaving for Paris. That is the extraordinary power of a real world brand: it is as powerful as the Cotswolds. This has to be good news for Stoke-on-Trent.

Nor have the other potteries entirely gone. Doultons is gone, now just a brand name at Wedgwood. But Spode, which might have disappeared, has been rescued by Portmeirion, who have brought the manufacturing of the archetypical Blue Italian pattern, among others, back from the Far East to their own factory in Stoke – hooray! Portmeirion itself powers on and also acquired the rights to produce the patterns of Royal Worcester. Then there are the sucessful Hotel ware manufacturers, Dudson, Steelite and Churchill , this last company also make domestic wares but not always in Britain.That is about it for the big potteries.

Smaller is William Moorcroft, where hand decorating of an extravagant and ebullient style is carried on at William Moorcroft, 60 ladies paint flowing neo-Art-Nouveau fancies to be snapped up by eager collectors worldwide.

Moorcroft is a profoundly special case. If any pottery company in Stoke could be called a craft pottery, this is it. In fact its owner, Hugh Edwards, describes the business as a creative industry and not a pottery, justifying this with the fact that only 7 per cent of the finished cost of the piece is the clay, the rest being value added by the craftsmen and women of Wm Moorcroft. Edwards is no potter – until he acquired the business in the 1980s he was a partner in a London legal practice – but he was a major collector of the company's polychrome wares and seeing it in trouble bought the business, in partnership with the publisher Richard Dennis.

The Moorcroft factory was founded in 1913 by William Moorcroft. He had attended both the

Wedgwood Training Institute (later the Burslem School of Art) and the National Art Training School (later the Royal College of Art), and indeed had also studied in Paris, so he brought influences to his output that were decidedly external to the city.

In Lichfield Street in Hanley there is Emma Bridgewater, who came to Stoke, like Susan Williams–Ellis, to find industrial-scale craftsmanship but a generation later employs 120 workers, of which more anon . . .

Then there is a group slightly smaller still. Caverswall still makes 1,000 elegant bone china plates a week; Aynsley and Duchess employ 50 people apiece; Burgess and Leigh is staving off extinction in Middleport, as we have seen (page 40). In Burslem, Wade employs 200 people who turn out tens of thousands of ceramic whisky bottles (good business for a century, although the strange high-gloss furry beasts of the cereal packet, the 'Wade Whimsies', have gone), and Royal Stafford another 75. Leedsware makes pierced cream earthenware. The group also includes Hudson and Middleton, and several others.

And there remain perhaps a hundred tiny potteries making beer pulls, figurines of gothic horror or mugs with laughing Labradors and grinning Staffies, employing ten people or fewer, but in aggregate a significant proportion of those in the industry and the skills it has maintained.

While the industry is much reduced from its 1970s heyday, it is still the greatest concentration of ceramics manufacture in the world.

THE "SPODE" LETTERING was put up in 1972 by DEREK LOWE

The CHIMNEY contained a BOULTON & PAUL ENGINE

Spode

This is one of three chimneys at JAMES KENT. It is still in action (The factory) and produces FRIT, ground glass, for the NUCLEAR industry

GLADIATORS
GYM

THE POTBANKS

The industrial city or town is not a popular model. We still prefer ports, villages, market towns and cathedral cities – in fact almost anything is better than industry. But there is a loveliness about the raw, rude utilitarianism of buildings whose main claim to fame is fitness for purpose. The net sheds of Hastings, the Kentish or indeed Hampshire oast houses, the engine houses of 'Improved' farms in the north (those octagonal or round buildings that housed the horse- or donkey-driven 'gins' that crushed grain into animal food), toll booths along the eighteenth-century British road system or the great medieval threshing barns through whose wide doors the wind would rush, winnowing the threshed corn prior to storage – all these are examples of buildings where function dictates form and where any subsequent decoration of stylistic addition is purely that, a grace note added as an afterthought.

The super-functionality of these buildings lends them a specific innate architectural dignity without any actual self-conscious architectural input, but despite the purist's desire for utter and uncluttered functionalism the addition of decoration can raise that industrial building to the sublime. Paddington Station, for example, is an outstanding structure in terms of engineering brilliance, but that extraordinary set of train sheds would be incomplete without the gothic cuspings and mouchettes with which the great iron members are decorated, making, in Herbert's words, 'drudgery Divine'.

Whether one's preference is for the clean lines of the pylon or the more decorated language of the Eiffel Tower, the industrial buildings of an area can become part of its vernacular. Vernacular building is that which is specifically of a place, in that it conforms to the building

tradition of that place, reflecting local conditions, both economic and geographic, and uses materials that are locally available. In its truest sense this definition excludes most industrial buildings, as they are products of a period in history when the transport systems that are needed to sustain an industrial economy are in place. The establishing of a network of canals, roads or railways not only allows goods or raw materials to be easily transported from place of manufacture to market but as a side effect also facilitates the travel of building materials. This means that materials that are relatively cheap to produce in one region, like Welsh slate, could be transported to areas where they were never found before, for example Stoke-on-Trent. This results in a breaking-down of regional variation as national norms are adopted and makes regional variation harder to identify.

Consequently Stoke-on-Trent, which is hugely if not entirely a product of the industrial age, has many building types that are standardized industrial models. For example, the terraced housing differs little in form from that in Derby, Leicester or Rugby and more significantly can be seen in Norfolk or Somerset in a recognizably similar style, differentiated only by slight changes in colour of the local brick. Now, of course, even this mark of identification is lost, as new housing is as likely to be comprised of elements manufactured in any part of Britain or indeed other European countries. Similarly larger domestic buildings, such as the terraces of higher-status housing for managers or master craftsmen, right up to the villas and smaller country houses of the Pottery owners, are quite national in character. Yet it is in the Pottery buildings and to a lesser extent some of those municipal buildings funded by their proprietors – the latter, of course, martyrs to the vicissitudes of nineteenth-century eclecticism – that the Stokishness of Stoke buildings manifests itself. And nowhere is this better illustrated than in the bottle kiln.

The characteristic bottle kiln features in the earliest illustrations of commercial potteries in Stoke. In fact this sinuous and decidedly female form is not the unique property of the Staffordshire potteries, and it can be found wherever pottery has been made – in Bristol, in Kirkaldy and even surviving albeit in a truncated form off the New King's Road in London. But it is in Stoke that it came to dominate whole city. In 1913 there were 1,200 such kilns and this continued to be the case until 1956, when the Clean Air Act spelled their death sentence. Some factories had a lot of kilns. In 1833 at Spode's Stoke factory there were at least twenty. Earlier still an illustration of the Brick House or Bell Works in Burslem, occupied by Josiah Wedgwood from 1762 till 1773, shows five kilns; eighteenth- and nineteenth-century representations all feature admirable ranks of copiously smoking chimneys. Later at the beginning of the twentieth century the chimneys and the pall of oily smoke that they generated had acquired a sort of celebrity status and picture postcards were printed by the thousand with droll titles like 'a fine spring day in Staffordshire' or 'a bright morning in Smoke on Trent'. These were, in reality, not exaggerating. A hundred years before an observer had described in amazement the effect of salt being thrown into the ovens (a way of forming a simple glaze then prevalent) during the synchronized firing of all of Burslem's kilns on a Saturday morning:

This occasioned such immense and constant volumes of smoke, as literally to envelop the whole neighbourhood: and it was not infrequent for passengers to mistake their way and run against each other during the continuance of this process. The scene which presented itself upon these occasions has been not inaptly compared to the emissions of Etna or Vesuvius.

A bottle kiln worked in the following way. The bottle-shaped form or hovel is only the external casing of the building. Inside is the kiln proper, a brick structure constrained by iron bands called bontings. These were essential, as the heating and cooling of the oven occasioned great movement in the brickwork. The bricks and the mortar that bound them were carefully composed to withstand these extreme conditions and the varying grades of firebricks employed were specified in

elaborate detail by the pottery owner. At the foot of the oven were a series of firemouths, from eight to eleven, which would be fuelled with coal.

Inside the oven the pottery, whether biscuit or raw clay pieces, was stacked within fireclay containers called saggars. This meant that the pots did not come into direct contact with the flames. It was the manufacture of these, carried out by a team under a master, each with his closely defined duties, that gave rise to the endlessly comical job description of saggarmaker's bottom-knocker. The saggars, the size of a shallow tin bath, were fitted one above another in teetering towers and stacked with terrific care by the kilnmen, an average kiln containing about 2,000 of them. This was not only a tricky job but a responsible one, as financially a lot rode on this process. An accident – and accidents were not uncommon – meant serious loss.

When the fires were lit, the furnace man would live in the kiln or immediately outside for the duration of the firing in appalling conditions of sweltering heat. His work place was between the inner and outer skin of the kiln. Each firing consumed 29 tonnes of coal, which represented a great deal of shovelling. The coal itself was important, as different grades could produce better or worse effects. Sulphurous varieties were potentially damaging, as were others with tendencies to form a solid mass of cinder difficult to remove once the firing was complete. Firing was a long job: from the lighting of the fires to the removal of the cooled ware could be from four to fourteen days.

The kilns themselves varied terrifically. Although all bottle shaped, the bottles could be either hock or burgundy (never claret); some narrowed steeply, others more gradually; and although they were utterly functional the builder could rarely resist some decoration at the neck – simple brick bands, dentils or even arcading. Josiah Wedgwood found this opportunity to decorate and enrich hard to resist, writing, 'I do not know where I should stop building hovels and that they may be decorated with Fascias, blank windows & Co at very little expense.'

Nor at his pottery did he resist the temptation to decorate the factory itself. He began to build his new model factory, Etruria, in 1767. The principal range was a distinguished building; indeed it was perhaps a more sophisticated one, or at any rate a more decorated

one, than his own house, Etruria Hall. The building was thirteen bays long and in three storeys the central bay projected beneath a dignified brick pediment. The ground floor was divided from the upper two by a sting course, and in the central bay this supported a generous Diocletian window and above it a tripartite window. Over the pediment was a graceful lantern. To today's eyes the design of the whole range feels less like a factory and more like the stable block of a country house. Indeed the architect, Pickford of Derby, favourite of the Lunar Society of which Wedgwood was a member, had worked on country houses in the area. Etruria became the model for the 'Improved' factory, improved at any rate on the main street frontage. Further back the muddle of irregularly shaped workshops and conflicting ranges of buildings, often with the kiln hovels protruding from the roofs, predominated.

Charles Dickens's description of the city in the mid-nineteenth century as 'A picturesque heap of houses, kilns, smoke, wharves, canals and river lying as was most appropriate, in a basin' captures the architectural muddle that defined it, but the great façades, from twenty to forty bays long, continued to appear, wreathed in approximate classical splendour.

Later factories departed from the ancients, adopting elements of Gothic or Byzantine architecture. By the beginning of the twentieth century the factory had ceased to attract decoration and a dreary descent through single-span roofs, rucked up in characteristic rows, led to the featureless and ugly sheds that now serve almost any commercial or institutional use, from giant-scale pet shop or sofa showroom to steel works or boatyard, barracks or sports hall and are now the normal form for what new pottery buildings.

A scattering of bottle kilns remain like scattered columns in a ruined forum as a reminder that Stoke's industrial architecture was specific and extraordinary.

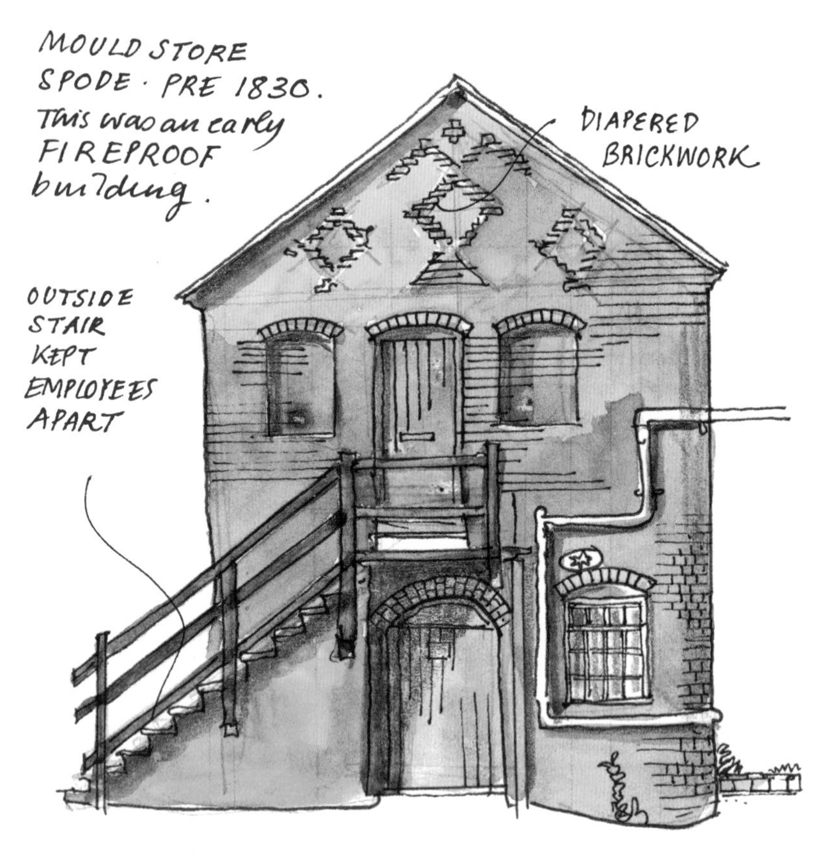
MOULD STORE
SPODE · PRE 1830.
This was an early
FIREPROOF
building.
DIAPERED
BRICKWORK
OUTSIDE
STAIR
KEPT
EMPLOYEES
APART

PAINTED on the WALL of PRICE & KENSINGTON
TEAPOT
CORNICE with
DENTILS
STRING COURSE

SUTHERLAND WORKS, AYNSLEY'S factory of 1861. VICTORIAN but Still ADHERING to the GEORGIAN Model.

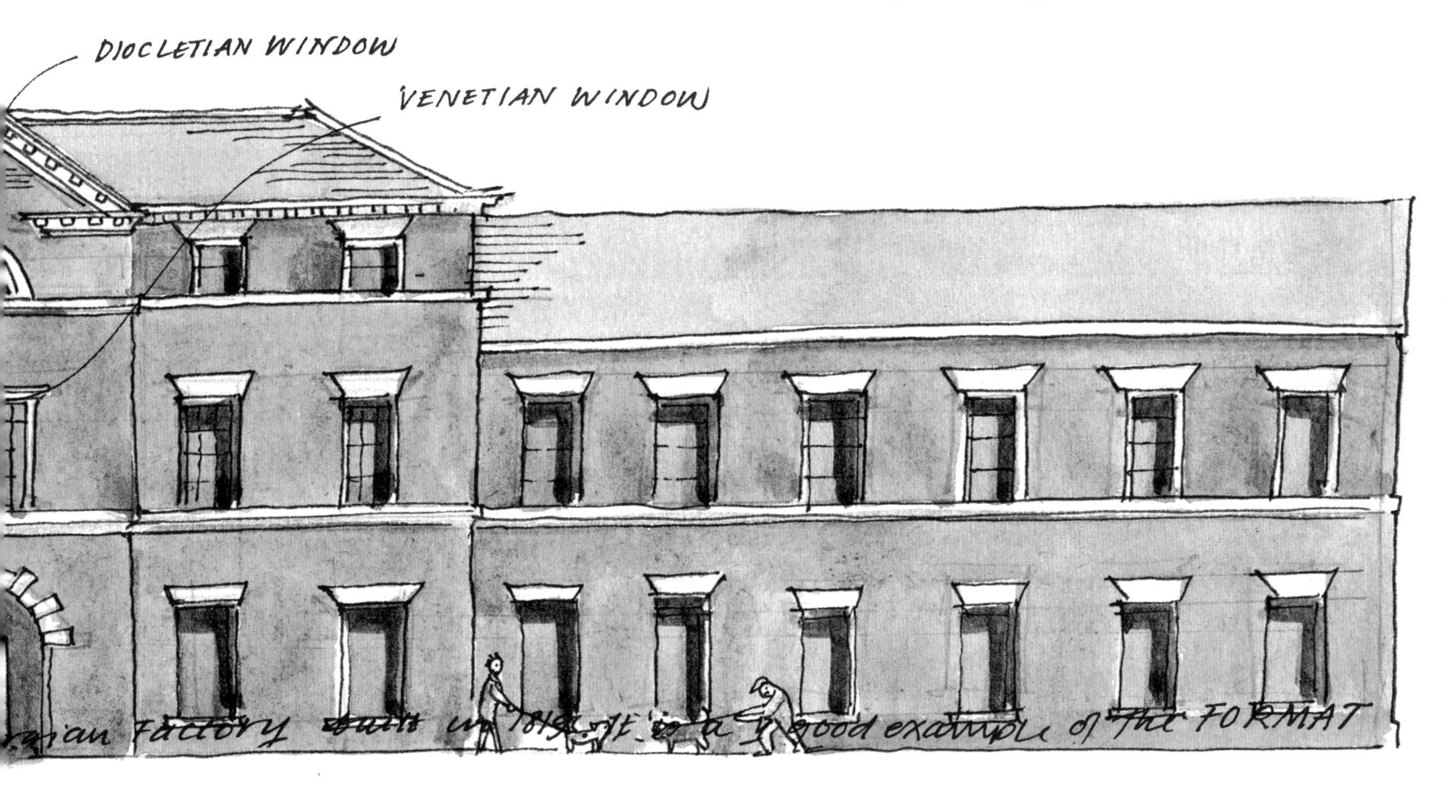

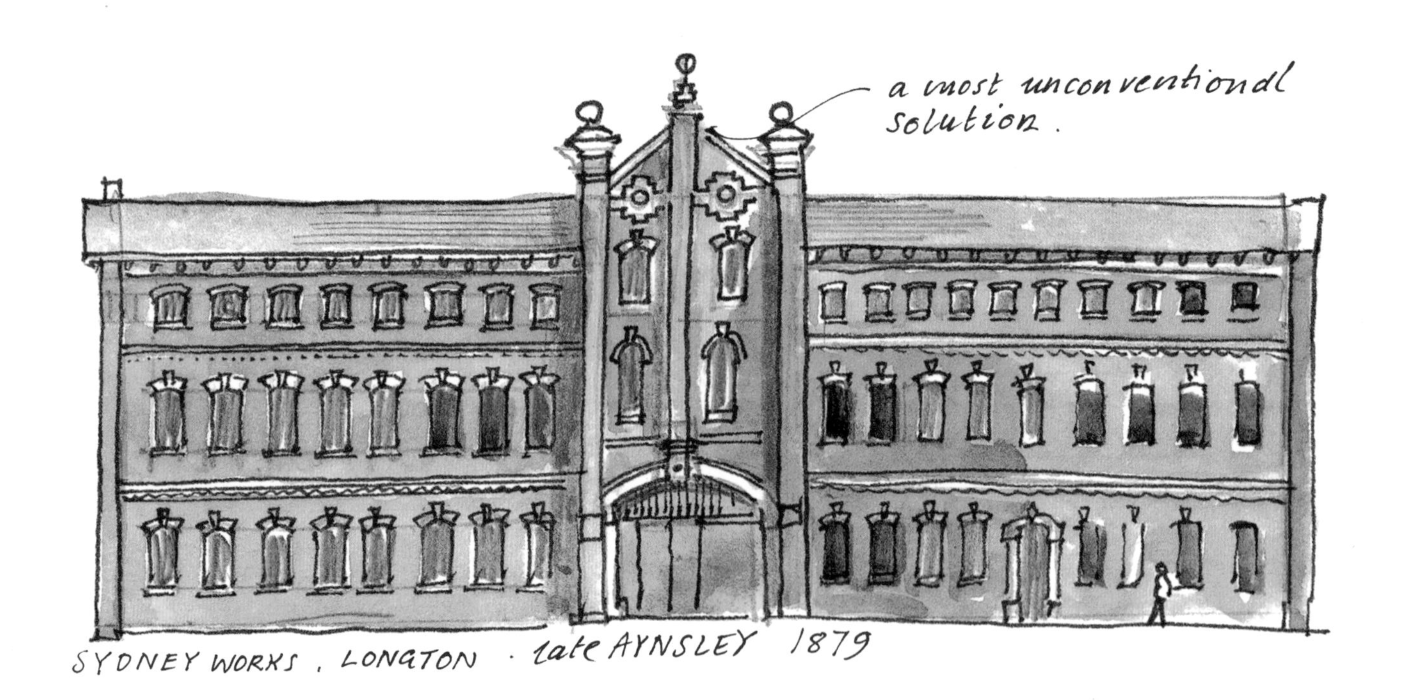
a most unconventional solution.
SYDNEY WORKS, LONGTON · late AYNSLEY 1879

STRUCTURAL POLYCHROMY @ NILE St. EX DOULTON (locally listed)

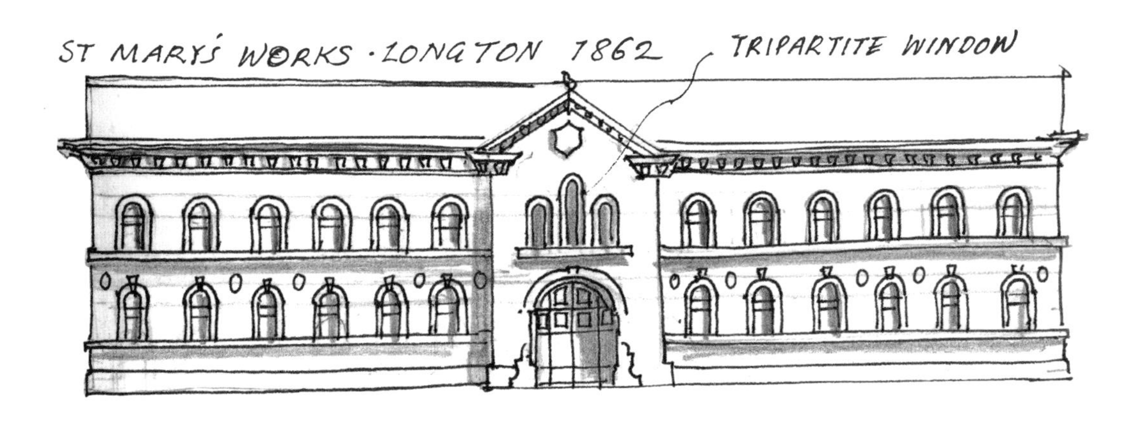

CHILTON St HERON CROSS

OLD DECORATING SHOP · SPODE · Early 19 · STOKE

ENSIGN WORKS · LONGTON · SHORT St
This whole complex – factory, pub + cottages – is now owned by the COUNCIL. There are PLANS for it to become a centre for Building TRAINING... fingers crossed.

It is mid (19) and LISTED grade II. The tall Hovel (Bottle) was for a Calcining Kiln

THIS SITE FEELS LIKE A FILM SET

PREVIOUSLY SHOWN. COMMERCIAL St LONGTON. THE HEIGHT & STRANGE FORMAT of this FACTORY, TALL and CONCISE, MAKES it REMARKABLE AS WELL AS HIGHLY VISIBLE from the Road

THERE IS LESS TO WORRY ABOUT HERE THE GLADSTONE/ROSSLYN WORKS COMPLEX · IS PART RESTORED AS MUSEUM & PART OFFICES · THE GROUP OF BOTTLES @ the Rear are like a BULGING FORTIFICATION SEEN AGAINST THE BLANK WALLS

PERHAPS BOTTLE KILN HOVELS are SO INSTANTLY APPEALING as they look so like a CHILD'S SAND CASTLE?

ACROSS THE ROAD from St JOHN's BURSLEM
THESE TALL CHIMNEYS are the remains
of ACME MARLS, BOURNE BANK. ALL AROUND
IS DESTRUCTION

J. KENT. FENTON.

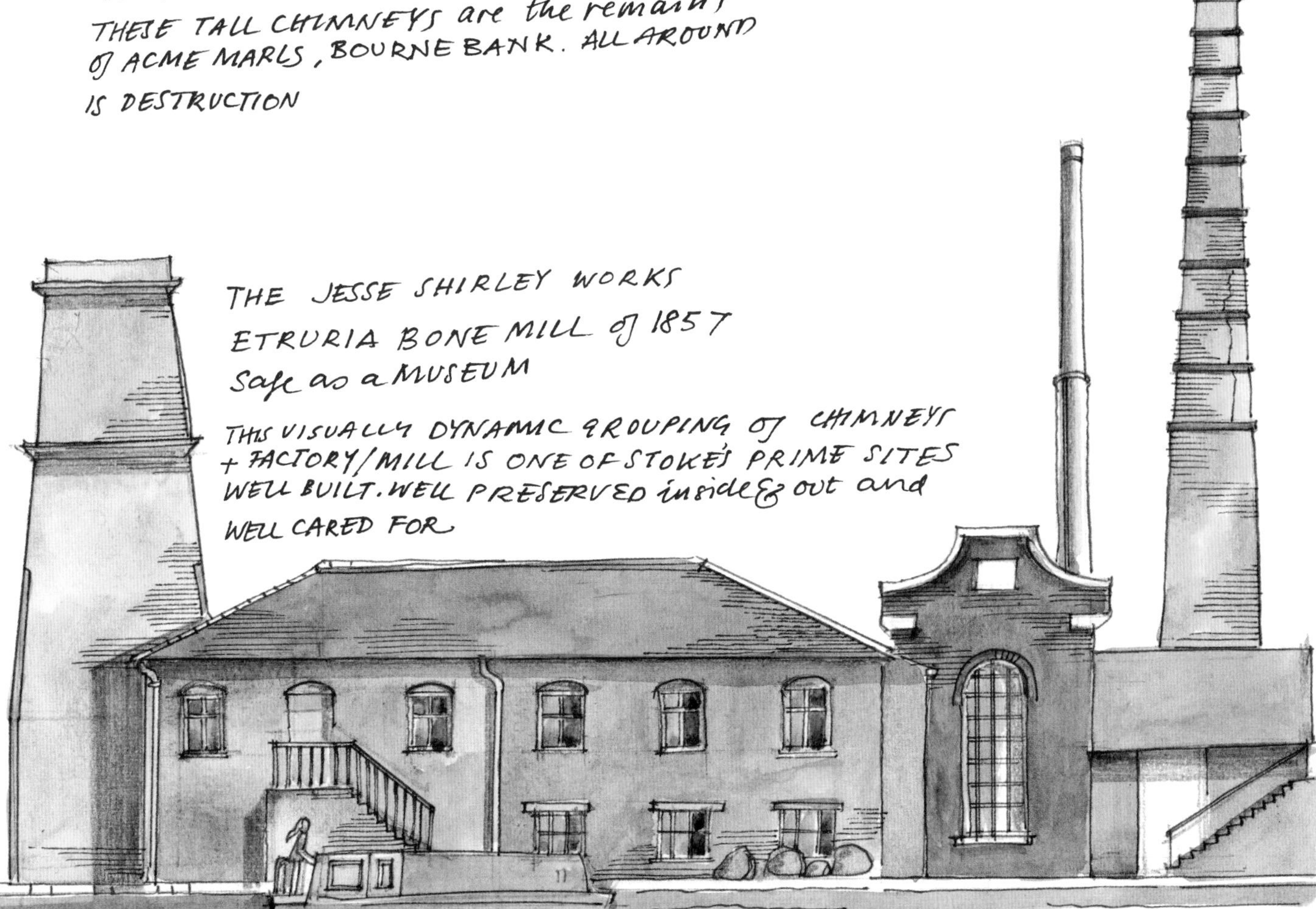
THE JESSE SHIRLEY WORKS
ETRURIA BONE MILL of 1857
Safe as a MUSEUM
THIS VISUALLY DYNAMIC GROUPING OF CHIMNEYS
+ FACTORY/MILL IS ONE OF STOKE'S PRIME SITES
WELL BUILT. WELL PRESERVED inside & out and
WELL CARED FOR

AMBROSE WOOD LIVED & WORKED in REGENT ROAD HANLEY. HE WAS A TILE MAKER (see Below)

HERE IS his MONOGRAM CAST as PART of The INVENTIVE DOORCASE to his house

BOUNDARY WORKS · LONGTON

THESE INTERLOCKING "D's" are PART of DOULTON's NILE St WORKS

This is A·WOODS Tile works with a HOARDING of TILES made ON SITE ·

CLIFFE VALE POTTERY
SHELTON NEW Rd.
THIS is FULL-BLOODED
LATE VICTORIAN
ECLECTICISM. 1887
of untraceably mixed
Architectural
antecedents
THE SITE HAS BEEN
REDEVELOPED, leaving
the FAÇADE
PRESERVED
CLIFFE VALE
POTTERY
CLIFFE VALE was the works of THOMAS TWYFORD

snow hill · STOKE Rd
V. EARLY 19

CANAL

Stoke is not really on Trent.

The Humber bridge, Britain's best and biggest suspension bridge, crosses the river Humber at Ferriby, connecting Lincolnshire, East Anglia, with Yorkshire, the North. As you drive over it the shimmering silver-brown river seems as wide as it is long, for it comprises not just the Humber but also the Trent, itself joined by the Yorkshire Ouse, a river that has in turn swallowed up the Nidd, for a great nation-draining final tidal flow into the brown North Sea. But 110 miles inland the Trent is a trickle. It winds through the middle of Stoke, but it is so negligible and its once-reedy bank so occluded by brick, stone and concrete that it has no impact on the city. Nevertheless, until the little river enters the lush meadows before Trentham, it flows through the city that bears its name. The endlessly repaired A500, which takes the visitor into town from the M6, follows its route. (It could not be said to trace it, as that would imply delicacy and care.)

But there is another waterway through the city: the Trent and Mersey canal and its sinuous branchline, the Caldon, follow the low grounds through Longton, Stoke, Hanley, Burslem and Tunstall. Until the 1950s these took coal, ironstone, clay and pottery from one factory or mill to another, quietly and safely. Along their length were frequent wharves, although most large factories had facilities of their own. Wedgwood's Etruria works had two separate fingers of water projecting into the middle of the factory to reduce road traffic, which meant wagon or packhorse, to the barest minimum.

To get the finished goods from an eighteenth-century pottery to Piccadilly in London before the opening of the Trent and Mersey in 1777 was a strenuous exercise. It was necessary to cover the 30 miles to Willington, at which point the Trent became navigable, by horse on uncertain roads. From there the load could travel by river to Hull and thence to London by sea. Similarly export wares bound for America had to cross 20 miles of Shropshire to Bridgnorth before the river Severn could accommodate the boats laden with crates of pottery headed for the port of Bristol. Canals and pottery were a particularly good marriage. What better way to bring in something bulky and heavy or to ship out the well-packed but delicate finished ware? Even the chalky-fragile biscuit ware could be transported this way in safety from one factory to another establishment for decorating or gilding.

With Josiah Wedgwood at the forefront of the body of investors who lobbied Parliament for a Stoke-on-Trent canal, a bill was passed at Westminster in 1766. It was the engineer James Brindley who designed and realized the waterway. With thousands of Irish navvies (navigation canal workers) he achieved this work in eleven years. While the Trent and Mersey canal was built at the huge cost of £300,000, it quickly repaid both investors and customers, for whom the cost of delivering their wares to the port of Liverpool dropped by 90 per cent. By 1795 the canals were so busy and the queues at the seventy-five locks so long that a plan for a new canal broad enough to take barges 14 feet wide was afoot. Conflicting interests stymied this new route, but an extension to the canal, the Cauldon, was cut at that time. By the nineteenth century it was anyhow too late for great expansion of the inland waterway system, as railway mania had broken out all over Britain. Here is Brindley's bathetic obituary in McGonagall-like doggerel:

JAMES BRINDLEY lies amongst these Rocks,
He made Canals, Bridges, and Locks,
To convey Water; he made Tunnels
for Barges, Boats, and Air-Vessels;
He erected several Banks,
Mills, Pumps, Machines, with Wheels and Cranks;
He was famous t'invent Engines,
Calculated for working Mines;
He knew Water, its Weight and Strength,
Turn'd Brooks, made Soughs to a great Length;
While he used the Miners' Blast,
He stopp'd Currents from running too fast;
There ne'er was paid such Attention
As he did to Navigation.
But while busy with Pit or Well,
His Spirits sunk below Level;
And, when too late, his Doctor found,
Water sent him to the Ground.

Suffice it to say an industrial accident and ensuing soaking led to his eventual demise.

The Potteries canals survived the railway's arrival, but the post-war road development programme and the introduction of cheap, fast road transport were the end of the barges. In 1990 a lone barge was moored at Johnson Brothers' works at Eastwood. It had recently been used to take ware to and fro from Barlaston or other Wedgwood factories and for the odd school trip. But by 1994 when Emma Bridgewater took over the site the barge had been spirited away and it was not seen again until it resurfaced as a floating restaurant many miles of still grey water away.

The canals, though, are far from dead. All day in the summer brightly painted narrow boats, some in the rather corporate liveries of boat-hire businesses around the Midlands and others in more far-fetched attire, travel the canal network. Stoke does not have a bad name among narrow boaters: after the flat green meadows of the Midlands or the cheaply brick-bright canalside quarters of Birmingham, the gritty industrial feeling of the city is truly foreign and so exciting. Attractions right on the canal include the Etruria Industrial Museum with its gruesomely graphic bone-crushing mill. (The millstones that smash the calcined flint or great white bones of Dutch cattle are not tidily carved millwheels but rude and gross rocks, too hard to shape, that smash the bones with a random cruelty.) Further along is the marina at the Festival Park. This rather gloomy spot in the midst of the ex-garden festival development, where Toys R Us rubs tawdry shoulders with Morrisons and Pet City, is watched over by *The Spirit of Recovery*. This is a particularly unlovely sculpture of a swan escaping from steely flames, a guileless reference to the Shelton Bar Steelworks established by Earl Granville in 1830 and abandoned by British Steel in 1998, on the site of which the park was built in 1986. It is, however, a safe place to moor your boat within reach of the city centre.

But as the old canal-facing factories are flattened, or as their owners euphemistically like to call it 'dropped', as if they were an unlearned H or some piece of ephemera and not a million bricks, a thousand panes of glass and a hundred thousand Welsh slates, the appeal of industrial Stoke to the boater may fade. After all, there are marinas and canalside parks in parts of the country where the air is sweeter and the views more bucolic. Again Stoke may be tidying away the heritage that can keep it alive. Stoke's industrial landscape is not a Hovis-advertisement fantasy or a rich man's amusement, nor a subsidized employment scheme or a theme park. This is what manufacturing in England actually means.

NEWPORT WHARF · NEWCASTLE Rd MIDDLEPORT
owned by British Waterways

DLP

Foley News
INSTANTS
OFF
LICENCE

HOUSING

There are some towns where housing goes beyond the purely utilitarian and where the house becomes an art form; Bath, of course, is top of the list with its skeleton of golden terraces, closely followed by Edinburgh, more serious and monolithic but still graceful. But these, like London, seventeenth-century birthplace of the English urban terrace, were cities with a large and powerful middle class, whether resident, as in Edinburgh, or transient, as in the case of the tenants for a season of Wood's crescents in Bath or Nash's in Brighton.

In an industrial town this is not the case. The nature of manufacturing industry in a pre-mechanized age is that there will be a very high proportion of operatives to managers or owners.

I might follow this with a deeply researched set of figures giving just those proportions in various industries and comparing those statistics with those of the clerk-to-partner ratio in nineteenth-century legal firms, with a brief reference to Mr Pooter and his expectations of suburban housing appropriate to a man of his standing, but perhaps that would be dull. What is definitely true is that the ceramic industry, while making huge advances throughout the eighteenth and early nineteenth centuries, did so in the field of technical innovation and not mechanization; so while the mules were rattling along the great cotton mill looms in Manchester or the woollen factories in Leeds the pottery operatives of Staffordshire were still working within their manual tradition. Thus the increase in production came as much from the huge influx of labour both from the surrounding rural area and, via Liverpool, from across the Irish Sea as from the perfection of such equipment as a patent cup-making machine (though of course these were to follow, from basic jiggers and jollyers in the nineteenth century to Wedgwood's robotic devices).

So there were many more workers than managers. And these workers needed housing as their population grew. In Longton, an area of later development, for example, the population in 1780 was 2,500; in 1811, 5,000 (10 per cent of the city's population); in 1830, 10,000; and by 1870, 19,000. Initially the pottery workers lived in existing or quickly built cottages. Few of those houses have survived, as is often the case with such buildings. Even in areas with available stone, early low-cost housing was as good as disposable, being thrown up by local builders or more frequently by future residents and their neighbours. The use of unseasoned or unsawn timber, with high proportions of quickly degrading sapwood, lath-and-plaster construction and under-fired brick, made the first pottery workers' accommodation no more resilient to the ravages of use, time and weather than a village house in India today. Roofs were of thatch and windows few and small.

As the industry grew and the need for accommodation ballooned, more and more labourers crammed into these cottages or subdivided houses. A series of sordid yards and lean-tos developed, providing insalubrious living conditions. Here the housing of the 1840s is described by T.H. Hawley:

The streets were narrow and contained many workman's dwellings, but these houses of the people had been erected regardless of size, form and order. A number of houses would be built right up to the narrow causeway, while the adjoining row would stand several feet back, just as it suited the sweet will of the builder, numbers of them ending in a cul-de-sac. If the houses had been discharged from the crater of some mighty volcano and dropped haphazard upon the land ready built, ugliness and confusion could not have been more pronounced.

This sounds – and early photographic evidence confirms that it was – every bit as squalid as Dickens's London, as illustrated in Gustave Doré's engravings of toppling slums; except this being in an area where space was at less of a premium (a situation that has never changed), the squalor spread laterally not vertically. Arnold Bennett (1867–1931), chronicler of the Potteries in his once nearly universally read and admired novels, described just one such hovel in *The Card* (probably the most digestible of his books as well as the shortest, for those wanting to try):

The solitary cottage had a front yard, about as large as a blanket, surrounded by an insecure brick wall and paved with mud. You went up two steps, pushed at a door, and instantly found yourself in the principal reception-room, which no earthly blanket could possibly have covered. Behind this chamber could be seen obscurely an apartment so tiny that an auctioneer would have been justified in terming it 'bijou', furnished simply but practically with a slopstone; also the beginnings of a stairway. The furniture of the reception-room comprised two chairs and a table, one or two saucepans, and some antique crockery. What lay at the upper end of the stairway no loving person knew, save the old woman who slept there . . . The only fire in the room . . . was in the old clay pipe which she smoked . . . She had lived in that residence for forty years. She had brought up eleven children and two husbands there. She had coddled thirty-five grand-children there . . .

The landlord, or in fact lady, of this cottage does not see maintenance as a major issue and indeed proceeds to attempt to evict the old lady resident; and this appears to have been not uncommon.

Local landlords, some benign like the Duke of Sutherland in Longton, kept cottages in good repair, frequently building new ones and let them at reduced rates to tenants considered reliable and of good character. The Duke of Sutherland's agents graded tenants according to a scale from 1, industrious, via 2, good, or 3, steady, down to 6, bad, paying particular attention to signs of incipient drunkenness, 'living with another man's wife' and other signs of moral turpitude. But other speculators produced cheap rows of hovels sure of a quick return on an all too modest investment. Sanitation was particularly undervalued by these slum landlords and despite severe overcrowding in the one-up-one-down or two-up-two-down buildings privies were few and far between. An account of Willow Court in Longton in 1850 describes

. . . a row of cottages at rentals of about 1s 8d per week; they have only one bedroom; men women and children all sleep in the same room. The privies are close to the cottages. There are five privies to the whole street of twenty five houses, some have neither back doors or privies . . . privies common to many family cease to be that which the name implies, and their use deadens all feelings of modesty and self respect in those that habitually frequent them.

There is little from the first quarter of the nineteenth century and still less from the eighteenth in the city of Stoke. An area that bucks this trend, however, is Longport around the canal. The Duke of Bridgewater pub, depressed but standing, commands the bridge. Across the canal lie the wharves, and opposite lies the decrepit but once-famous manufactory of Price and Kensington. The words 'PRICE'S NATIONAL TEAPOTS' are painted in bold sans-serif letters on to the brickwork of this building, in which the Prince Regent's dinner service for Brighton Pavilion was made. A part of this development survives: a short terrace of obviously early

cottages with steep roofs and substantial chimneys, now all shops, or they were so until recently – several are now boarded up. They are a visible reminder of what early Improved housing looked like in Stoke, and like so much else they are at risk.

So nineteenth-century artisan housing was grim; living conditions were basic, cookhouses providing the necessary facilities for those too poor to find fuel themselves, and the pottery owners were, to put it politely, winging it. Public outcry ensued and it comes as no surprise, therefore, to find in the late nineteenth century a new model of terraced house with proper drainage, cobbled yards behind and full provision of windows at front and back. These are the surviving form and, while for forty years many of them were fecklessly demolished, they still remain the most visually dominant type. When unbroken by improvement the sight of row upon row of these blackened brick terraces with slate roofs and brick chimney stacks is thrown into relief by the undulating ground of the five towns to provide Stoke's most evocative and characteristic view. In the post-war years these terraces have fallen out of favour, particularly with the local authority, for whom they have perhaps seemed a symbol of the past and one with bad associations. Many thousands of these houses have gone, replaced initially with bungalows and more recently with various forms of flat and house. Initially their loss was unlamented, but more recently there has been a realization that quite well-built houses are being replaced with rather flimsy ones that look glossy and glamorous when new but age less like a house and more like a car.

In fact a lot of post-war housing was built on the fringes of the city, leaving the centre to its own devices – a process that has saved many streets from destruction. These peripheral estates are lighter and airier than their terraced predecessors, but undistinguished.

Terraced housing is far from uniform, though. Some examples are entirely plain, with rarely even a trace of decoration, but in others, whether through the use of precast composite stone detailing or the use of polychrome brickwork or moulded terracotta, the urge to decorate has conquered utilitarianism. These higher-status streets are often associated with particular pottery owners, whose munificent nature extended

A ROW of V. EARLY (19 WORKERS COTTAGES. NEWCASTLE Rd MIDDLEPORT. These are some of

beyond the architectural enrichment of their factory façade and lodge to the housing of at least some of their workers. Herbert Minton was one of the first to build a first-rate model village near his own house, church and rectory in Hartshill above Stoke. Minton Cottages (1853) are a perfect group of mid-Victorian terraced houses with grand porches, gothic detailing and polychrome brickwork.

The streets around Victoria Place in Shelton are good streets of model housing erected for their workers by the Baker, later Meath Baker, family in 1887. Their company, Bourne, Baker and Bourne, had been potters in the area since the early 1830s and had a large factory in Shelton. They were the next year to continue their munificence with the building of the civic buildings of the town; these streets were the first step in that direction. Replacing poor-quality eighteenth-century slum dwellings, the houses had a larger ground plan and their own sanitary facilities. Inside, the rooms have fireplaces, another improvement, both downstairs and up; but despite being 9 feet 6 inches high, a feature visible from their elevations, the rooms themselves remain small in plan. In 1910, following southern examples, the Garden Village movement arrived in Stoke and one of the architects of Letchworth, the leading example of this utopian school of town planning, arrived to help. What resulted was Penkhull Garden Village, on 38 acres on a rise above Stoke, and a hundred houses, built at low density, appeared in a dilute Arts and Crafts style.

One special characteristic of Stoke's artisan housing that differentiates it from other northern industrial equivalents is the use of ceramic floor tiles, even in the most modest house. Joseph Minton and Co. was the world's leader in this field. Herbert Minton had collaborated with Augustus Pugin on his masterpiece, St Giles, Cheadle, producing the most elaborate and beautifully made multicoloured encaustic tiles for the floor of that great church.

Despite being fifteen minutes' drive from Stoke, this is worth a brief aside, as it is the great church of the Gothic Revival. Pugin, funded by his great patron and leading lay Roman Catholic the Earl of Shrewsbury, had his way entirely with this temple to liturgical reform and

innovative archaism. The wilder flights of this anyway peculiar architect here took wing and in achieving this inspirational exemplar of the perfect pre-Reformation church Pugin employed many of the technologies and skills produced by the Industrial Revolution he so despised. Foremost among these were those of Minton, whose growing palette of coloured clays and slips was to prove an important component in the sometimes lurid colour schemes favoured by his friend and collaborator. Chemical blues and rich oranges combine in designs gothic and cursive but of an accuracy and consistency never before attained – certainly not in the period so admired by Pugin. In fact the designs of the tiles themselves, when looked at individually, are quite simple, geometric and truly medieval in inspiration, but the effect of their massed presence and the relative absence of aged patina is noisy and hectic, particularly when combined with the stencilled wall painting, elaborate brocades and most skilfully wrought iron and brass.

The terraces of Stoke benefited from this fertile friendship (though in fact it seems that most of Pugin's relationships were more than a little fraught) and by the 1880s the output of the Stoke factory of J. Minton and Sons and its successor, Minton Hollins, was providing the porch and hall tiles for the city, not only for the floor but for the panels on either side of the internal walls of the porch, and in the clear bright colours that lift so many of these houses from the everyday. Another typical feature is the boot – or perhaps clog – scraper. This is built right into the fabric of the wall, a kind of scraper *in antis*. These scrapers were highly functional, as no housewife wanted the filth of the potbank, or indeed the street, walked into her spotless parlour. They have mostly survived the century since they were installed.

Factories also need managers and owners, and consequently there is another class of house in Stoke, although it is sometimes quite well hidden. There are few three-storey terraces in the city, but terraces or at least linear compositions of fine houses remain. One such is in Waterloo road in Cobridge. Unsurprisingly built in the years immediately following Wellington's popular victory in 1815 (much recorded in clay in the factories of Stoke, as flat-backed Staffordshire figures of the Iron Duke himself and other more utilitarian commemorative wares). This brand-new road connected the first-born, Burslem, with its thrusting and commercially powerful younger sister, Hanley. The route was marked with factories, chapels, churches and fine villas in various styles – neo-Tudor, Regency or Italianate, depending on the date and the leaning of the builder or future tenant. Some of these remain intact, with dainty cast-iron balconies and refined pedimented porches, while others, shorn of all decoration that a century of disregard could allow to drop, are just hulks, reminders that there was a villa here in 1820 and that for some proprietor of a factory this seemed for a time to be the place to hang his hat. Some even have an arched entrance beside the house to allow access for wheeled vehicles and all had large gardens behind.

Larger and slightly later buildings of a similar class face the cemetery in Shelton. These are again in an agreeably eclectic selection of styles – Grecian, Egyptian, Roman, Gothic or straight brick box – although all are of roughly the same construction date. Grand and sophisticated, they would stand up to any such street in suburban London (Clapham Common northside, perhaps).

They are in varying degrees of lovedness and mainly in commercial use.

The best of all the managers' enclaves is the Villas in Stoke, described on page 17. Some remain in fine condition, with children bouncing on trampolines and lawns mown, others are more threadbare; but the whole thing is both complete and powerfully evocative of the life of the upper echelons of the industrious classes in nineteenth-century Stoke.

Last are the great houses, and there are not that many at first glance. In Stoke the great houses mean pottery – but not in one case, as the really great house of the area, Trentham Hall, Barry's elaborate Italianate palace built for the Earls, later Dukes, of Sutherland, was demolished all too soon in 1910/12. Its ducal owner took flight to his recently cleared Highland estates, having taken exception to the waters of the youthful but ravaged river Trent, which had a habit of flowing whatever colour was most recently deposited in it from the colour factories a mile or two upstream; and while this colour was no doubt villainously poisonous, it was not a potent enough brew to cause the miasmic hordes of gnats and mosquitoes who favoured that bit of the Trent valley to curl up their flimsy little wings and die. So he left.

The landscape around the hall, however, 'Capability' Brown's improved and romanticized Trent valley, remains, as does the city's only Grade I listed building, the Trentham Mausoleum, built by Charles Tatham in 1808. This hefty Egyptianate shrine sits like a squat blackened temple, ignored, in a stand of trees on the left of the road to Stone. Opposite it a truly brutish and lumpen block fills the view, the Trentham Park Holiday Inn, and across its faceless car park Trentham village, a scramble of retail chalets grouped around the entrance to the restored lake and gardens form the bathetic end of that pleasure drome, Trentham Park.

The Sutherland family, holders of various titles – Earls and Dukes of Sutherland, Marquesses of Stafford, Lords Strathnaver, Earls Granville and various other Leveson-Gore derivatives – occur in street and pub names, and as donors of several halls, institutes and schools. They were immortalized as the Earls of Chell by Arnold Bennett; they founded steelworks (Earl Gower) and coal mines (Sutherland); and they controlled large parts of the freehold property of the city. The Lords Stafford, of a medieval barony, live at Swinnerton just outside the city and are unrelated.

The Wedgwood family built several seats, the first of them the Big House in Burslem, in the centre of town, which states quite unambiguously that they were cocks of the dungheap. It is proud, solid and altogether good looking, a confident Georgian big townhouse which has survived two centuries of institutional tenants to continue to command the entrance to the town from Hanley. Etruria Hall has already been described (see page 31).

The Leek, and later London, lawyer Thomas Mills commissioned Sir Robert Taylor in 1756 to build Barlaston Hall, a good tall Georgian country house in the park of which the current Wedgwood factory would later be built. This is, in the conventional view, the most architecturally distinguished building in Stoke and in a very good setting, its park falling away dramatically towards the river Trent (not at that time suffering from the noxious odours that would make it such a bad neighbour to the Sutherlands). It is a very fine house, with five bays and three storeys. The centre three bays project beneath a brick pediment with a central bull's eye window. Elegant string courses define the first and second storeys and the whole building, with two projecting one-storey bays on each side elevation, sits on a rusticated plinth, the basement storey, which houses the kitchens. As well as sitting most imposingly on its vantage point, it is built very beautifully. The soft pink brick, the fine mortar and the sharply cut dentilated frieze are all top quality.

What is most exciting is that in 1992 it was a wreck but was rescued by SAVE Britain's Heritage. It was then acquired by the current owners, who have thoroughly restored it inside (it has outstanding plasterwork in most rooms, all of which has been painstakingly reconstructed from remaining fragments, drawings and careful research) and out. Perhaps its most striking decorative feature, echoed in its white rendered lodge in the nearby village of Barlaston, is the glazing of the windows, in lozenges like a Chippendale frieze. Safe in private hands, it is still very easy to see from the old drive, which is now the public road from Barlaston to the Wedgwood Museum and factory.

The hall's near neighbour is the Upper House, another Wedgwood build, of 1858. This hotel – I recommend it (indeed it is frequently my home), it is the best in Stoke – was built as a house for Francis Wedgwood in 1858. Its elevations are in a watered-down Italianate style, the interiors in Jacobethan. This time, the style has inched away from the classical or indeed the Chippendale towards the wide-eaved and generous picturesque. It is an understatedly Italianate villa. An elegant portico *in antis* in sandstone – that is, set behind the face of the elevation – leads to a much compromised but quite recognizable country-house interior. This is available for all to see, as it is a hotel. A polite notice informs residents that in this house Ivor Novello once played the piano and, while it is no Gosford Park, that single fact somehow brings the building to life (it had a quiet patch as a home for the blind in the early twentieth century). Outside, some noble cedars, a beech tree and some better-than-institutional gardening give the visitor the faint but traceable sensation that they are in nineteenth-century Staffordshire.

(Should you need a brief antidote to post-industrial distress, you might enjoy a surprising bit of landscape five minutes' walk from the hotel. Go down the bank and turn left, following the footpath through a gate and an arable field, and at the top of a mild incline you come to Barlaston Downs, a great contrast to grimy Stoke.)

Both these houses are visible on the right-hand side of the train, if arriving at Stoke by rail; they are usually visible five or ten minutes after Stone and just before the tannoy announces that the station is five minutes away.

Wedgwood was not the only potter-builder. Josiah Spode II built a graceful villa with shallow domes and ionic pilasters called the Mount. And there are strange big-house remnants throughout the city: Ridgeway's house in Hanley, for instance, now the Mumbai Junction Indian Restaurant (also worth a visit if hungry), and the Masonic Hall near by. It is hard to imagine that the rough asphalt yard of the hall was once velvet lawns with shrubberies and a flint-lined walk leading to a pretty fretwork summerhouse with honeysuckle curling round the chamfered posts. It is not like that now: and in common with its contemporaries scattered around the city, usually in front of or very close to the factory to which they belonged, it is stranded, divorced from both its original *raison d'être* and its factory.

There are genuinely great houses elsewhere in Staffordshire: Weston, with its collection of paintings; Shugborough, with its extraordinary selection of temples; Ingestre, now a sad place, very institutional and the gardens in ruins, but with Sir Christopher Wren's church a treat; even the remnants of Alton Towers. There are also lesser ones: Hales, Oakley, Swinnerton and Chillington. The first group are open to the public, the last rarely. But these are of Staffordshire the county, not Staffordshire the Potteries, and so, while worth mentioning, are really diversions from the subject of this chapter: the domestic buildings which derive their main significance, architectural interest apart, when they are fitted in to the story of the Potteries, as the homes of the hundreds of thousands of craftsmen and women who made plates, cups and saucers teapots and gravy boats, platters and water jugs for the world and of the people who employed them.

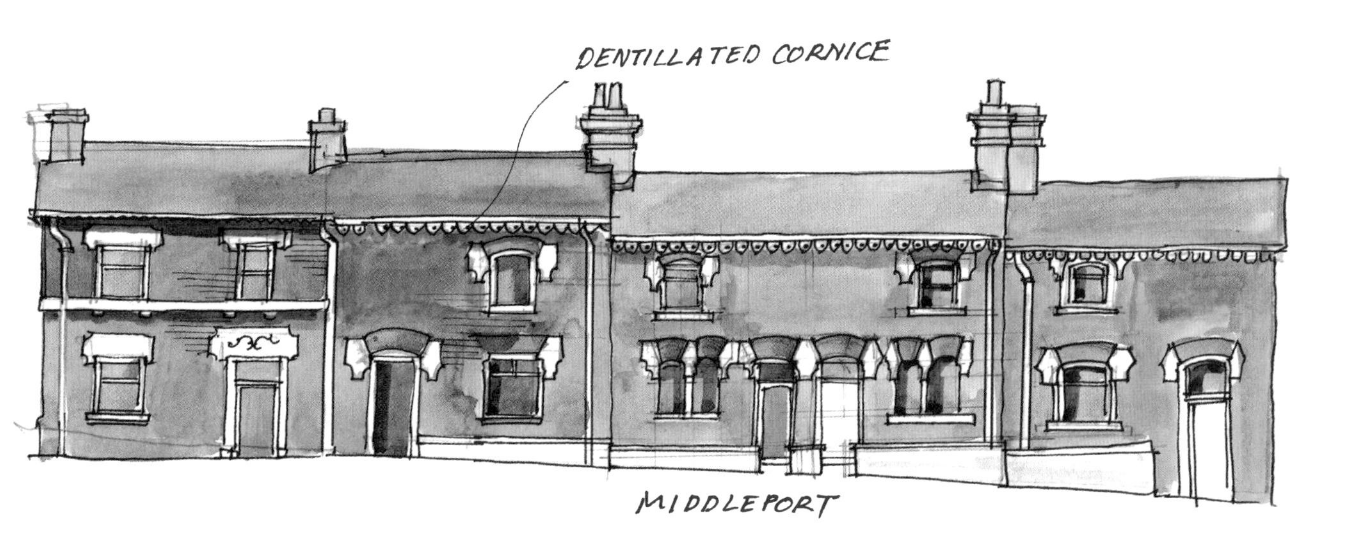
DENTILLATED CORNICE
MIDDLEPORT

MOULDED TERRACOTTA DECORATIONS
GAS OFF
A TERMINALY RUN-DOWN TERRACE in SHELTON · WILL WHAT COMES NEXT be HALF AS GOOD?

BOOT SCRAPERS
ARCH TO ACCESS ALLEY

CHURCH TERRACE FENTON · SERIOUSLY "IMPROVED" HOUSING . Late 19

HITCHMAN St · FENTON · BUILT by the MEATH · BAKER FAMILY · HITCHMAN was a Meath-Baker Aunt.

BLOCKING COURSE

CORNICE

N.B · This is HIGH-STATUS BUILDING in the CITY ∴ RARE

ELEGANT IRON BALCONIES

GRANGE TERRACE · WATERLOO Rd c1820 · This was site of RUSHTON GRANGE

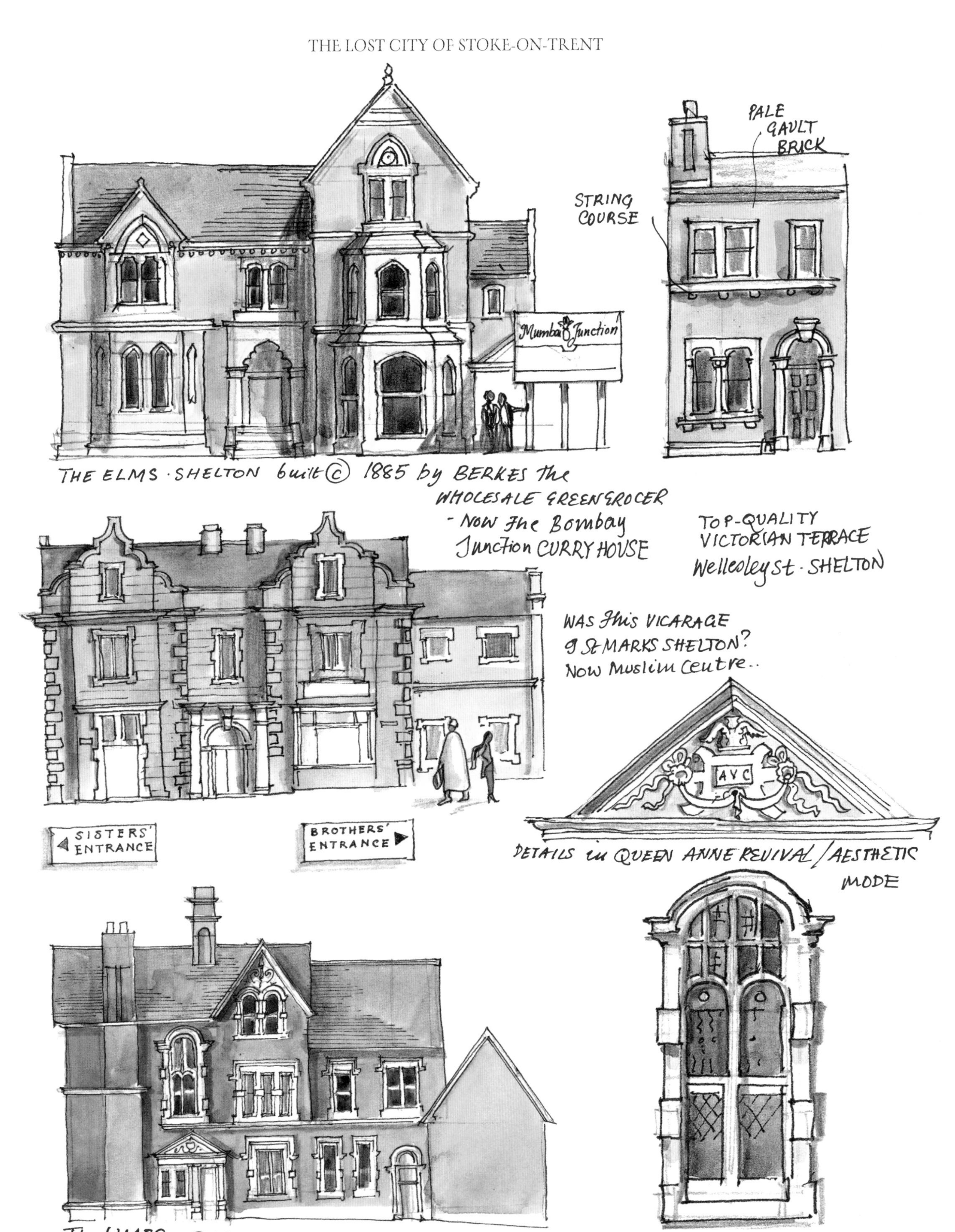
PALE GAULT BRICK
STRING COURSE
Mumbai Junction
THE ELMS · SHELTON built © 1885 by BERKES the WHOLESALE GREENGROCER - Now the Bombay Junction CURRY HOUSE
TOP-QUALITY VICTORIAN TERRACE Welleoley St · SHELTON
WAS this VICARAGE of St MARKS SHELTON? Now Muslim Centre..
SISTERS' ENTRANCE
BROTHERS' ENTRANCE
AVC
DETAILS in QUEEN ANNE REVIVAL / AESTHETIC MODE
The LIMES · PENTON was once RECTORY now REST HOME

FARMHOUSE at FORD GREEN
late C18 - TYPICAL TALL FARMHOUSE
of STAFFS/CHESHIRE

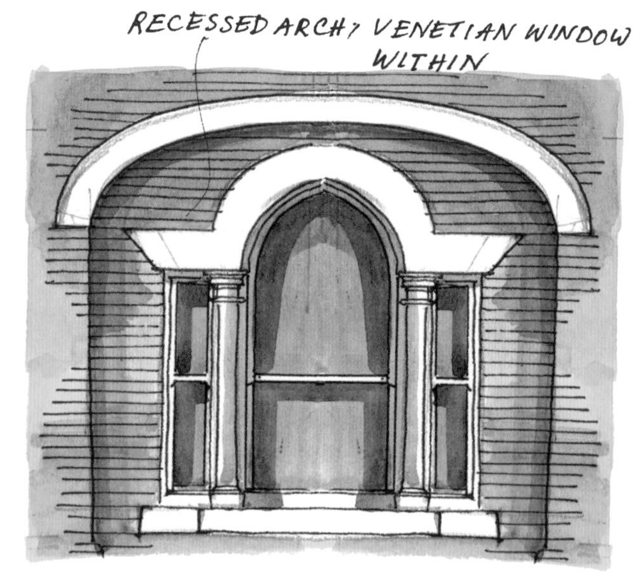

NEWCASTLE St. SHELTON
PORTLAND HOUSE 1832

THE UPPER HOUSE · BARLASTON ·
ONCE A WEDGWOOD HOUSE where
IVOR NOVELLO PLAYED the PIANO
AFTER SUPPER. NOW A HOTEL.

CEMETERY RD. HANLEY – 1870s/1880s

HOUSE at CANON St SHELTON. BUILT for THOMAS FORD CHINA MANUFACTURER 1860S. HEAVY VICTORIAN CLASSICAL

RICARDO ST · DRESDEN a FINE VILLA of APPROX 1865

(a notable Liberal)

THE PORCH IS ABSURDLY GRANDIOSE, OF DUBIOUS ARCHITECTURAL PARENTAGE & SPLENDID

MONETA HOUSE · RICARDO St 1865 · designed by R·C SUTTON Arch' of NOTTINGHAM

BARLASTON HALL · Built for LEEK & LONDON LAWYER THOMAS MILLS by Sir ROBERT TAYLOR in 1756 · TALL, FINE HOUSE, beautifully built in SOFT RED BRICK · IT IS THE CITY'S BEST HOUSE

When PEVSNER described the Hall in 1974 He bemoaned its parlous condition under the Stewardship of the WEDGWOOD Company. NOW it is a Shining example of THOROUGH but SENSITIVE RESTORATION under NEW OWNERSHIP

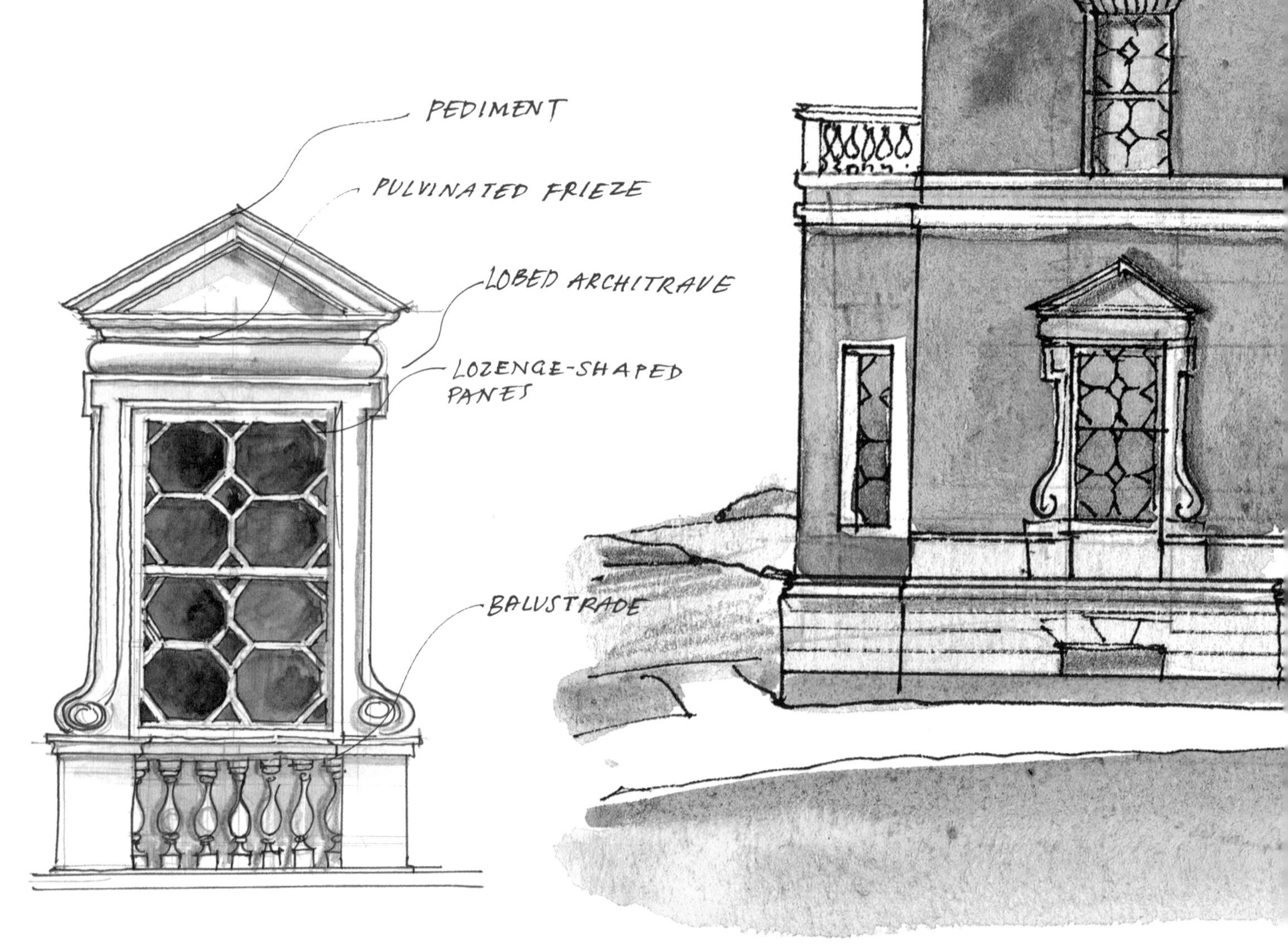

STRING
COURSE
PROJECTING
BAY
FRIEZE WITH TRIGLYTHS
TUSCAN COLUMNS
BC

PATHETICALLY INEPT DETAILING IN IMITATION OF....

... REFINED WINDOW at ETRURIA HALL

ETRURIA HALL · EPICENTRE of INDUSTRIAL REVOLUTION (1770) AND ITS GROSS NEIGHBOURING HOTEL

This is INSENSITIVE & INSULTING COMMERCIAL DESIGN..

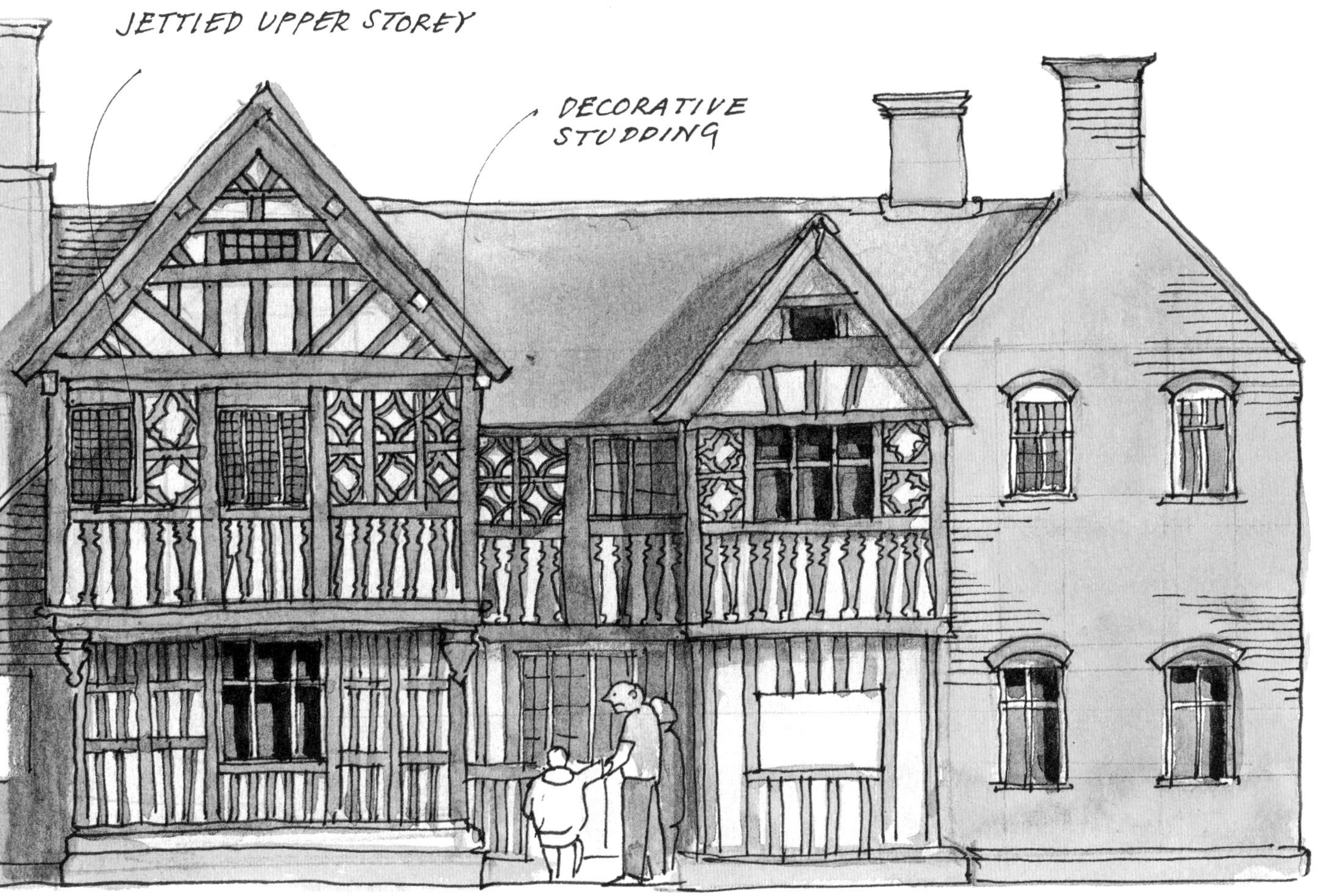

FORD GREEN HALL · SMALLTHORNE · JACOBEAN & GEORGIAN

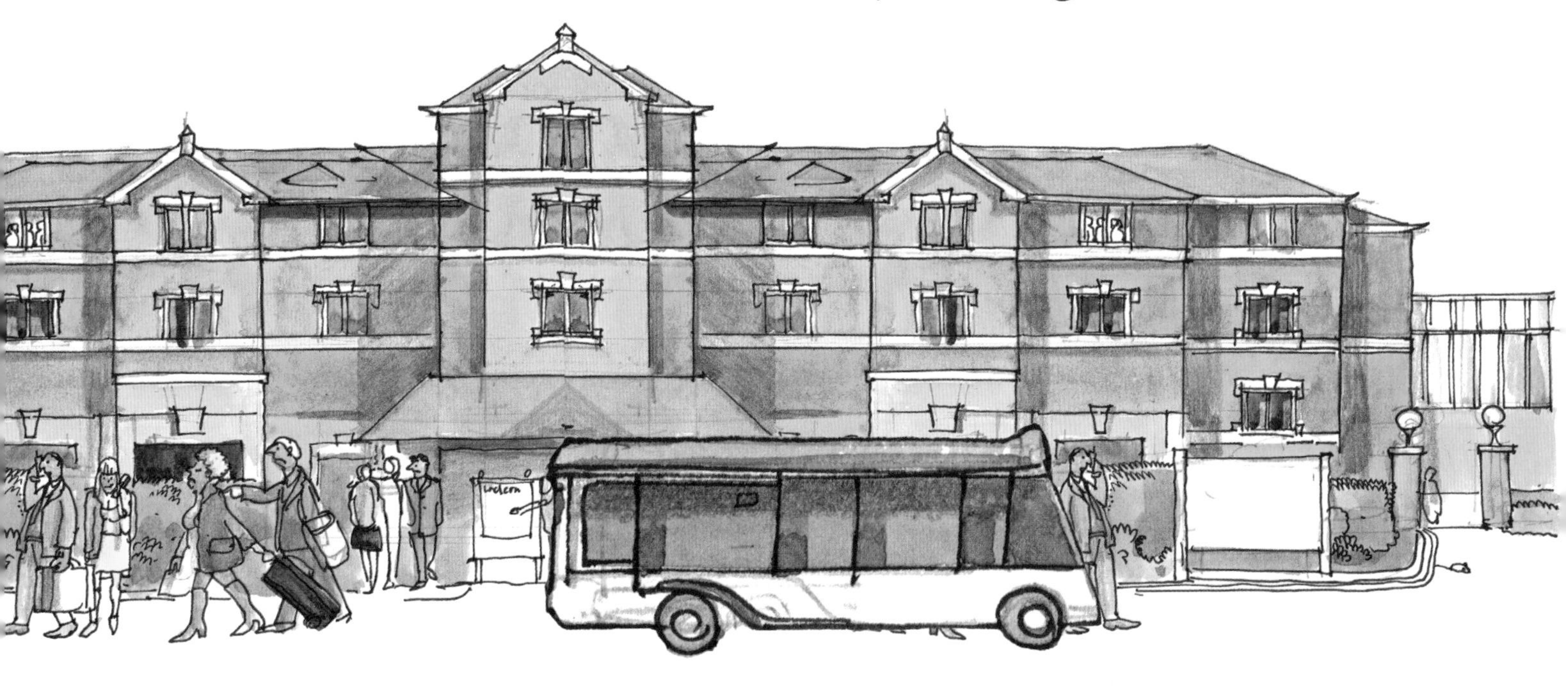

GRECIAN DETAILING IN
CEMETERY Rd HANLEY

STAINED GLASS + CAT IN HANLEY

VILLA in WATERLOO RD ·CORBRIDGE

The BIG HOUSE MOORLAND Rd BURSLEM 1751
Built for THOS & J. WEDGWOOD TUSCAN PORCH

T & J WERE UNCLES OF SIR J'S WIFE (& COUSIN) SARAH. IT was
FROM THEM THAT he RENTED The IVY HOUSE WORKS IN 1759.

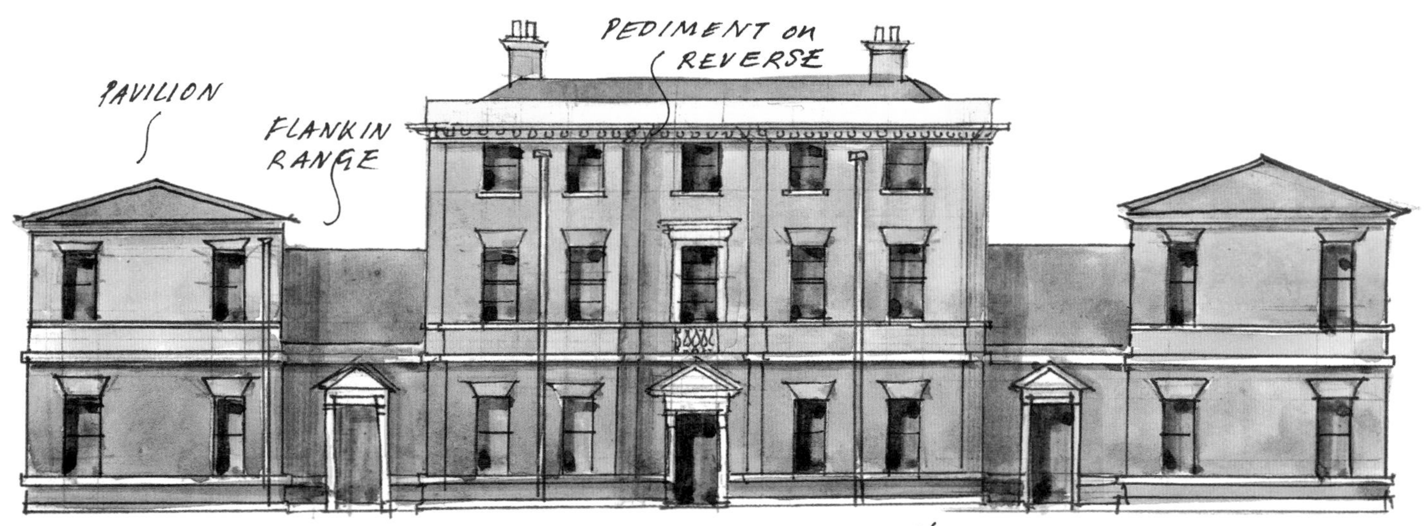

ETRURIA HALL – home of Sir J. WEDGWOOD – ARCH' JOSEPH PICKFORD of DERBY 1770

MUNICIPAL BUILDINGS

Stoke-upon-Trent is not short of public buildings. I have touched as lightly as possible on the whole six towns issue, as it feels like a family quarrel that eventually makes you hate the member who is your friend, but this is really the time for it. These are the barest facts, rehearsed again.

Stoke is the oldest and had one of the two parish churches. It became home to Spode's factory, a group of buildings that has dominated that town for over two hundred years, and more recently to that of Portmeirion. The main station and its hotel are also in Stoke, but the A500, a gouging new road of 1977 that wanted to be called the Queensway in honour of the Silver Jubilee but ended up plain and matter-of-fact as the D road, cuts it off from its nearest neighbours, Shelton and Hanley, the second town. These two are joined at the hip. To the south is Fenton, which is connected by a long strait (ish) road to Longton, known for Nonconformism and for being home to more factories than anywhere else. Burslem was home to the first potteries, so styles itself the 'mother town'; it also has the best town centre by far. Last of all is distant Tunstall. For various reasons – none of them interesting except that Stoke's greatest non-potting son, the writer Arnold Bennett, brought the whole multitown thing to the public eye by publishing *Anna of the Five Towns* and thus firmly planted the seed of five – when the proto-DVLC decided that car number plates must not just say HRH1 or similar and should refer, albeit in coded form, to the place of registration of the vehicle, Stoke was awarded the VT prefix (later suffix), the V representing the Roman V for five and the T for towns. In case you have never noticed, this system still works, so Norwich cars say EX, Carlisle AO, Chichester HO, Hull AT and so on. (I have now revealed both my main geographical points of reference and a pathetic and childish ability to remember number plate detail . . .)

The excuse for repeating my description of the towns is that the sixness of them means six of everything – six libraries, art schools, town halls, law courts and market buildings – which in a city with a huge preponderance of small terraced houses and mainly defunct factories is probably just as well.

With the possible exception of the grimly Doric Tontines, the old market hall in Hanley, the various public buildings on Burslem and perhaps Longton town hall, these are not of actual architectural significance, but they are all of interest, not least because one is able to compare one to another. This very comparison was also central to their conception. There is, of course, no need at all for each

borough to have such huge buildings to house their administrators. Longton and Hanley are just 4 miles apart and that great journey is anyway easily broken at Fenton; Burslem is less than 2 more short miles up the road from Hanley and Tunstall is contiguous with Burslem. Yet all these relatively modest industrial towns boast the richest law courts, institutes, libraries and town halls. This is the result of competitive notables of each town vying one with another for supremacy and status as capital of the Potteries. While this may have been innocuous enough in 1890, it has now produced an *embarass de richesse* of great public buildings, nearly all of which have become, or could quite easily be proved to be, redundant. Some are benefactions, like the square at Fenton, composed of church, town hall, law court and bank, the direct gift of the Meath Baker family, once the principal manufacturers of that place. Others are the product of more general civic expenditure. Some are also in better condition than others.

Burslem School of Art, a gift from the Wedgwood family, stands behind Burslem's main square and with its neighbour, the Wedgwood Institute, epitomizes the best of nineteenth-century philanthropy. Its lofty studio windows light the rooms in which generations of the better class of ceramic decorators, and sometimes designers, were trained. A one-year course here provided the initial training needed to sustain the generally high level of skill found in Stoke. On the ground floor municipal magnificence is expressed through the great public rooms and stairs, while at the back survives a second-floor greenhouse that once housed the floral models on which botanical illustration relied. Standing in the main studios one is eye to eye with an image of Sir Josiah, complete with artificial leg. On either side of him are terracotta discs, or tondi, illustrating in heavy relief the months. All these and the elaborate structural polychomy of the façade are testaments to the extraordinarily high

KING'S HALL · STOKE 1911

POST OFFICE · BURSLEM 1937

standards of Victorian work. Perhaps working and learning in these august buildings had an effect: it may have proved them fit for purpose, imbuing in the students a feeling and respect for design and craftsmanship. The art school is much restored, and is now home to various institutions from a recording studio to a signwriting school, while the institute opposite, another Wedgwood benefaction, is in a parlous state, despite its architectural splendours.

Tunstall, described by the architectural historian Pevsner as being 'no more than one really urban street', is dominated by its own Victoria Institute (now Tunstall Public Library), an oversized and under-articulated block that oversees the tangle of over-engineered road development that chokes the town. More refined is the clock tower of 1893, gift of Sir Smith Child, which like a cadet Big Ben tries to proclaim Tunstall's greatness.

More recently buildings have been erected by the city as a whole. The library is an austere but elegant building in the Art Moderne mode, which is acquiring distinction with age. Less lovely is the hulk of the city museum, now called the Potteries Museum & Art Gallery. It is a building that only its designer or perhaps his mother could love, a Brutalist lump, impervious to its surroundings and in no way hinting at its marvellous contents. Its façade is embellished with a clumsy frieze in heavy relief alluding to the city's heritage in an unsurprising and inelegant idiom. It is, however, a visual delight when compared to the millennium shame of the city. Ceramica was a serious and well-meaning attempt to interpret the existing ceramic output of the remaining Staffordshire potteries to visitors and schoolchildren. It has not been a success and has left a visually intrusive reminder of this, an incomprehensible clutter of post-modern steel and glass building components thrown together in a fashion no doubt intended to express a forward-looking and dynamic approach to industry but that now seems both too provisional and tragic. Its plate glass is grimy, the café inside is deserted and the shop fittings of the abandoned commercial enterprise it contained lie shipwrecked and in full view. Worse still, this sorry ruin is attached to the imaginative and fantastic Burslem Town Hall, which dominates the town's square, the best-preserved architectural passage in the city.

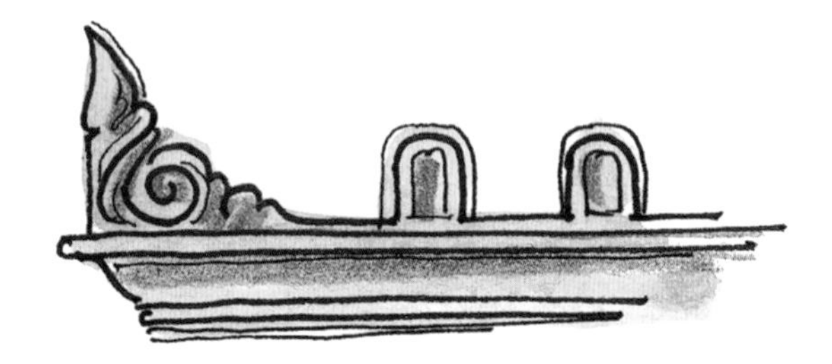

This
ANGEL is the subject
OF A SONG by ROBBIE
WILLIAMS, STOKE'S
GOLDEN BOY
THIS WAS BURSLEM'S
SECOND TOWN HALL,
BUILT IN 1854 by
G.T. ROBINSON.
EBULLIENT 19 CLASSICISM
A. BENNETT ENTHUSIASTS will spot
DENRY AND The COUNTESS of CHELL

The TOWN HALL · HANLEY · was built as the QUEEN'S HOTEL · 1869 + BECAME Town Hall in 1884. Built in the style of a LOIRE CHATEAU

THE OLD SHAMBLES OR MEAT MARKET · HANLEY. BUILT IN MUSCULAR DORIC IN 1831. NOW KNOWN as THE TONTINES. LOTTERY TICKETS to fund EMIGRATION WERE SOLD HERE. Later in the C19 STOKIES settled in POTTERSVILLE, WISCONSIN + TRENTON · NEW JERSEY

FENTON TOWN HALL – NOW LAW COURTS, a Gift of the MEATH-BAKER family 1889.
(PEVSNER CALLS it "PORTLY"!)

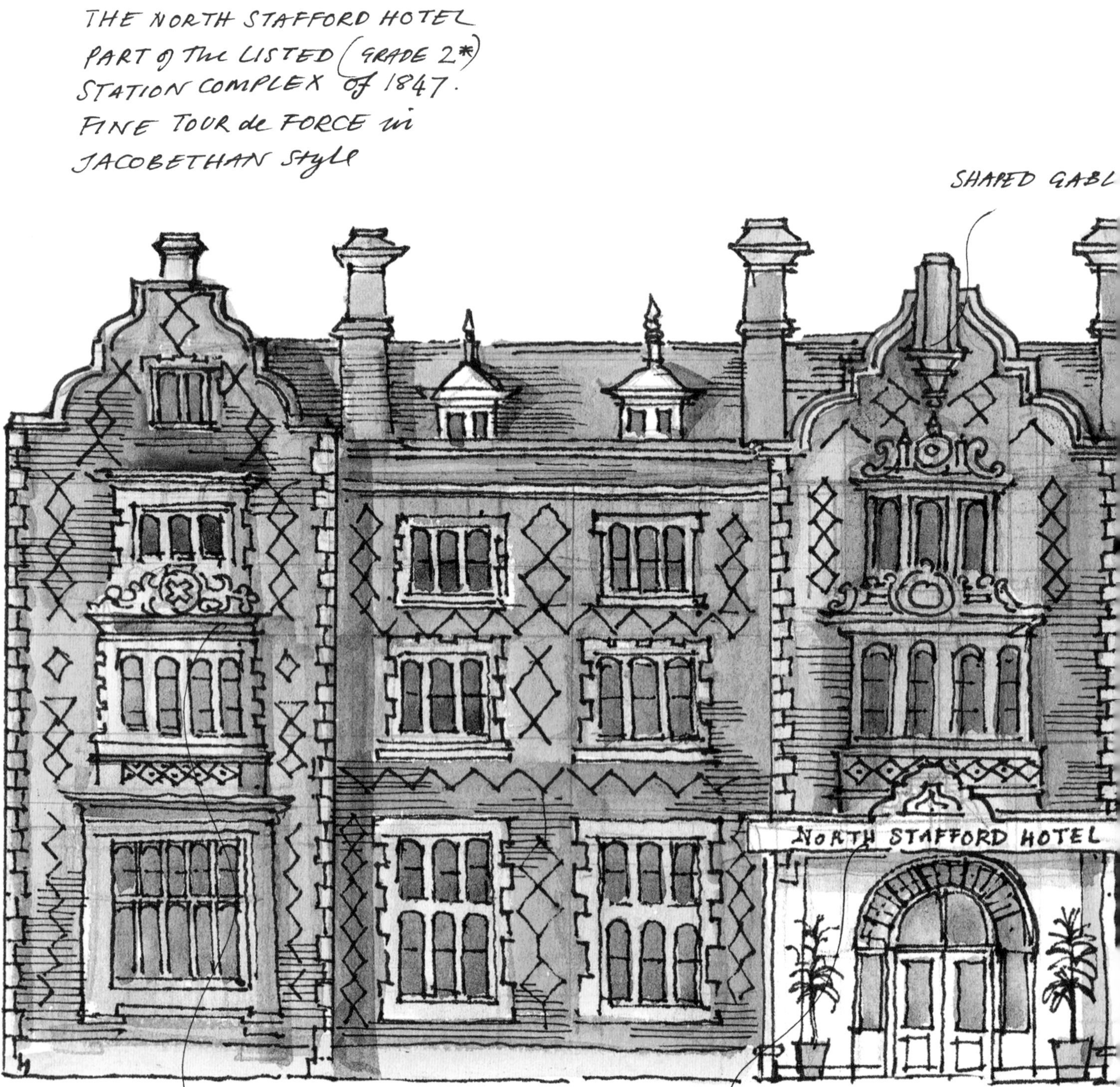

THE NORTH STAFFORD HOTEL
PART of The LISTED (GRADE 2*)
STATION COMPLEX of 1847.
FINE TOUR de FORCE in
JACOBETHAN Style

SHAPED GABL

NORTH STAFFORD HOTEL

STRAPWORK

DISMAL PORTE COCHERE REFL

DIAPERED
BRICKWORK
CTS DIMINISHED STATUS

OPEN PEDIMENT

SHOP IN HANLEY. in VENETIAN GOTHIC (much DILUTED). RUSKIN MEETS STOKE on TRENT

BUILT as the BARRACKS in 1897 THIS BECAME a COUNCIL TRANSPORT DEPOT

STAFFORDSHIRE & POTTERIES WATER BOARD 1860
Heavily decorated & with much tiling. Until fairly recently this housed a RESTAURANT and perhaps will again

. It has found CONTINUED USE as an ENGINEERING WORKS

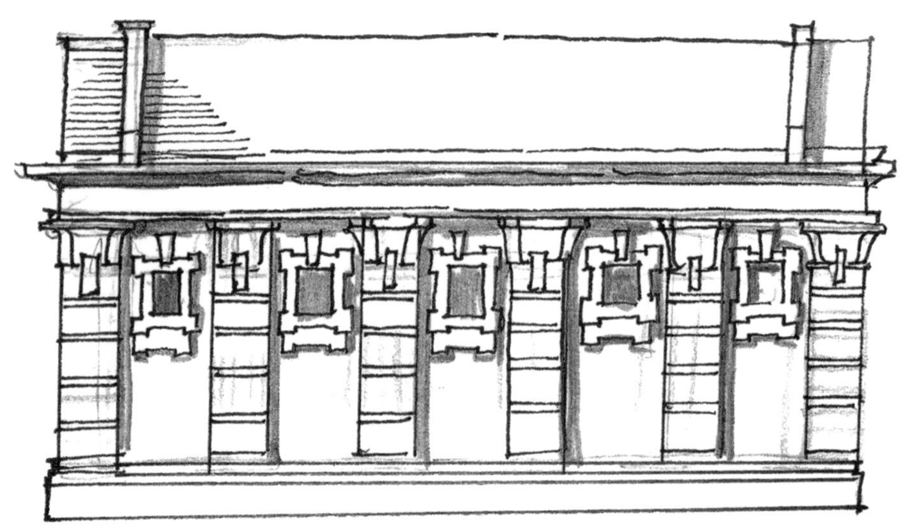

IN 1873 HANLEY'S PUBLIC BATHS DEMANDED THEIR OWN SUBSTATION. Here it is but the final plug was long ago pulled in the (demolished) BATHS

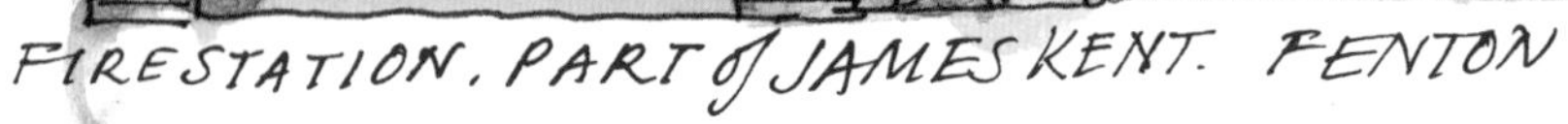

FIRESTATION. PART of JAMES KENT. FENTON

THE WEDGWOOD INSTITUTE was built in 1869. ORIGINAL DRAWINGS by G.B. NICHOLS were ADAPTED by J. LOCKWOOD KIPLING. The ARCHITECT so admired the LOCAL BEAUTY SPOT of RUDYARD LAKE that he named his SON after it....
WITH ITS TERRACOTTA PANELS, MOSAICS & POLYCHROME BRICKWORK IT is ONE OF The CITY's MOST STRIKING BUILDINGS. BUT... It is in poor repair particularly Within.
MOSAIC ZODIAC PANEL
TERRACOTTA RELIEFS X12
SCORPIO
OCTOBER
DEPRESSED CULTURE LOVERS

HANLEY POST OFFICE 1906, REMINISCENT of BUCKINGHAM PALACE but situated, as it is, in a narrow st this view is never seen. It is currently empty

POST OFFICE WINDOW AEDICULE, in BEST EDWARDIAN BAROQUE (POSTMEN are imaginary)

RENAISSANCE DOORWAY

SPARE MODERN STYLING ON The CITY LIBRARY 1968-70...

...nearby The POTTERIES museum was similarly elegant until The Brutalist, Brick-clad additions of the 1980s destroyed it.

BLINK & YOU'LL MISS IT. THIS IS SLATED for DEMOLITION

A LIGHT-HEARTED & JOLLY FAILURE - SHOPPING CENTRE & BUS STATION 1970s

THE WEDGWOOD MUSEUM IN BARLASTON has an AWARD-WINNING COLLECTION. IT IS an ATTRACTION that SHOULD NOT be MISSED but while it is housed in a smart INTERIOR. the EXTERIOR is in the style of a contemporary SERVICE STATION. This PORTRAIT of J.W in GLAZED ENGINEERING BRICK IS BEYOND A JOKE.

WEBBERLEY'S BOOKSHOP. LATE (19). This elevation makes a virtue of REPETITION.

THE MAIN WASTE DISPOSAL INCINERATON WELCOMES VISITORS TO STOKE
And is built to a BOLD, FUNCTIONAL & PLEASING DESIGN

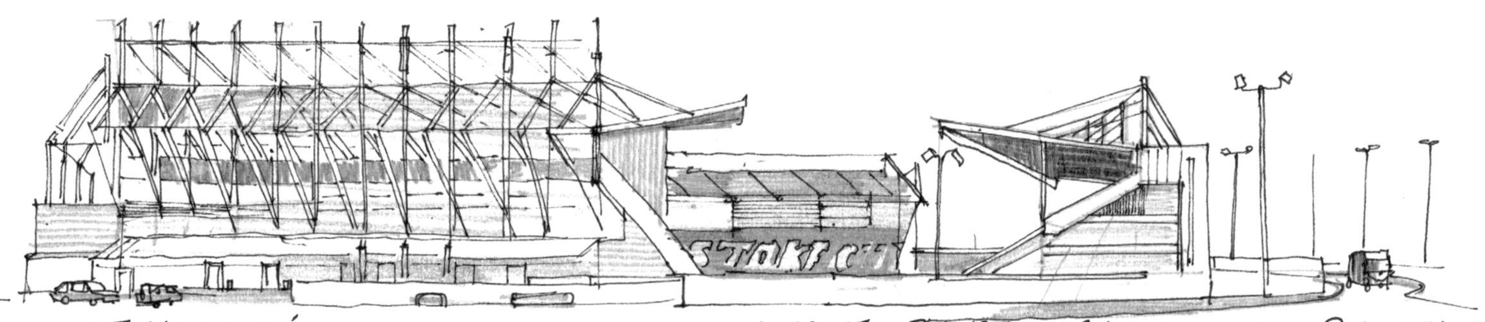

STOKE CITY'S FOOTBALL GROUND of 1997 - FUNCTIONAL, POPULAR & WITH
NO SILLINESS

THE WEDGWOOD MUSEUM 2007 & PART of The FACTORY 195?

DUKE OF BRIDGEWATER

THIS PUB in MIDDLEPORT was once a house & Part of DAVENPORT's FACTORY

THE GEORGE, BURSLEM
once full of visitors with Pottery Business

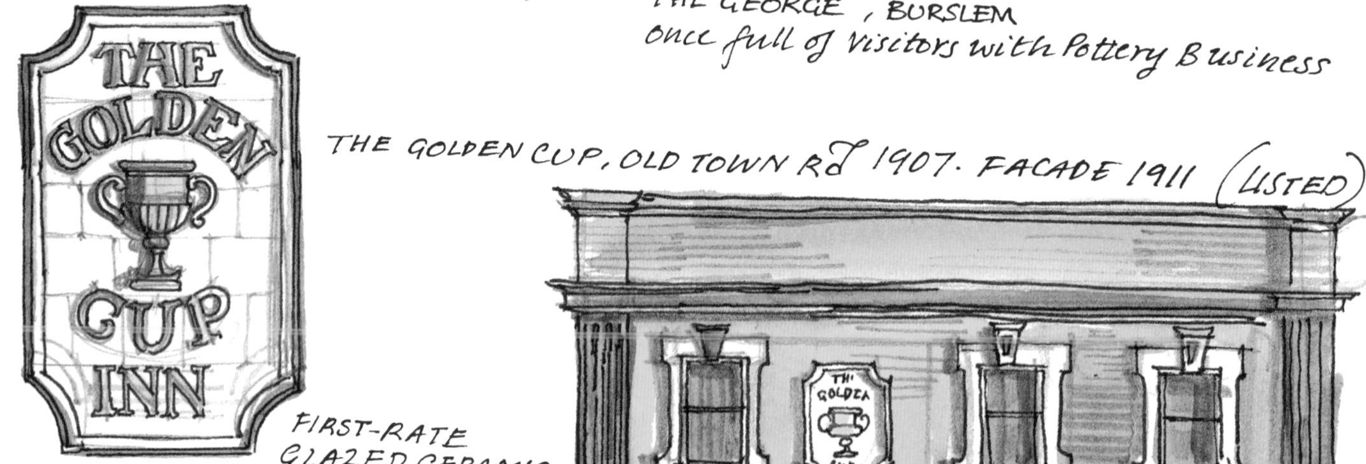

THE GOLDEN CUP, OLD TOWN Rd 1907. FACADE 1911 (LISTED)

FIRST-RATE GLAZED CERAMIC FASCIA

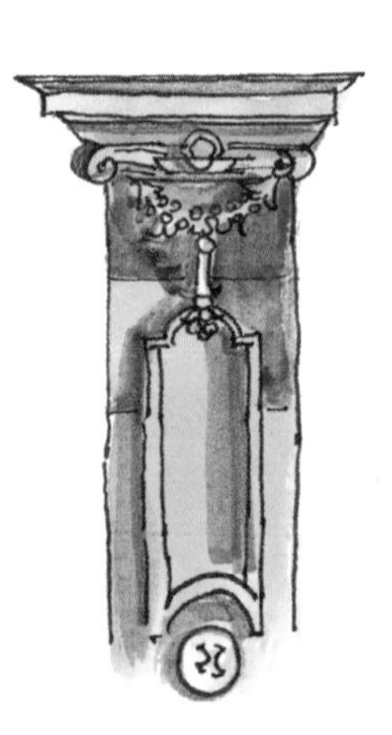

THE AMERICAN PUB · WATERLOO Rd 1815-1817
NAMED for the craze for US-bound EMIGRATION in 1834.
AMERICA WAS IDENTIFIED with an ESCAPE from the POVERTY
of the POTTERIES. SADLY MANY EMIGRANTS RETURNED
DISAPPOINTED.

THE LEOPARD IN BURSLEM. In 1765 J. WEDGWOOD
Thos BENTLEY. ERASMUS DARWIN & JAMES BRINDLEY
AGREED to INITIATE the TRENT and MERSEY CANAL

FRONT 1830 – THREE-STOREY BOWS

PUB SIGN (in Relief) for BEAR & BELL

THE PLAIN & UNADORNED NORFOLK INN was hurriedly created from the first three terraced houses available that did NOT belong to The tee-totaller factory owner J. RIDGWAY

* BOOTSCRAPERS REVEAL where the HOUSE DOORS once WERE!

THIS PUB (the BEAR & BELL) IS UNDER TOTAL THREAT. AN IMAGINATIVE & INVOLVED ESSAY IN OLDE ENGLISH...

WAR MEMORIAL
ALBERT SQUARE
FENTON
1919
MEMORIAL TOWER in TUNSTALL
PARK to:
WILLIAM ADAMS: HELD LAND
in TUNSTALL 1307
RICHARD ADAMS · COALMINER
1487
WILLIAM ADAMS · WORKED
a POTTERY NEAR HERE
1597
JOHN ADAMS · CHIEF
CONSTABLE of TUNSTALL
MANOR COURT 1616
WM ADAMS · POTTER
1777 – 1805
WM ADAMS of
GREENFIELD
1833 – 1905
MONUMENT to CHARLES MEAKIN
builder of the EASTWOOD WORKS

SUTHERLAND INSTITUTE
AND FREE LIBRARY
UNCHARACTERISTIC OUTCROP OF ART NOUVEAU
GIFT OF THE DUKE OF SUTHERLAND
WATERSTONES
DETAILS @ KINGS HALL
H. POST OFFICE DOORWAY
BLOCKED PILASTERS
1950s EDUCATIONAL OPTIMISM - HANLEY

The POTTERS FEDERATION HQ: WINTON St 1935 – RESTRAINED ART DECO

The QUEEN'S HALL
BURSLEM built by Alderman Sydney Malkin in the hope of re-instating
BURSLEM as Principal town of the five...

Dual
carriageway
SEVERN
TRENT
WATER

CHURCHES AND CHAPELS

That the church is the most important building in a village or town goes without saying. Or does it? In any village the church is hard to rival; it is the repository of all local history, the most significant building in architectural terms and often the largest and oldest surviving as well. In a market town it may have a rival in terms of scale, perhaps a town hall or arcade, but this will be unlikely to be of more architectural significance, unless the church is a very dreary nineteenth-century rebuild or has been seriously damaged at some time. Cities have much more to offer in the way of public buildings and these – guildhalls, city halls or other institutions – may be distinguished and designed by fine architects, but in most cases the church with which they have to contend for supremacy is a cathedral and so a hard act to follow. But in the case of a city or town that is as purely industrial in character as Stoke-on-Trent places of worship must take second, or even lower, place.

Pevsner, in his Staffordshire volume of *The Buildings of England*, adheres to his usual churches-first approach in the Stoke-on-Trent entry, which begins:

The five towns are an Urban tragedy. Here is the national seat of an industry, here is the fourteenth largest city in England and what is it? . . . mean towns hopelessly connected now by factories, by streets of slummy cottages or by better suburban houses. Here is no centre to the whole, not even an attempt at one and there are not even in all six towns real local centres.

Then he lists parish churches and Nonconformist chapels, noting that there are no medieval survivals. There are several reasons for this. One is that these settlements were of little or no significance before the Industrial Revolution; indeed only Burslem and Stoke were originally parishes. Those churches and chapels that did exist were perceived by the leaders of the new industrial towns as being insufficiently sumptuous for the borough's increased importance, which resulted in rebuildings. A final reason is the high incidence of subsidence due to earlier coal-mining activities in the area. Such subsidence throughout infirm Stoke has affected many buildings. The Infirmary in Etruria, for instance, which was built in the 1850s, was already condemned by 1874, when it was rebuilt at Hartshill, as the ground it stood on was fast falling away, because of previous mining workings. However, the problem has frequently been used as justification for extensive demolition, allowing perfectly good buildings to fall to the wrecker's ball.

Pevsner does, however, refer to eighteenth-century survivals and perhaps none is more impressive in conception, yet so pathetic in condition, as St Paul's, Hanley. The bare facts of this church's history are that a new church was built at the expense of John Bourne on a site given by John Adams in 1738, so already two great pottery families were involved; and that it was swiftly rebuilt in 1788. That rebuilt church is the current one. Its tower can be seen peeping through the later buildings of Hanley as one circumnavigates the city centre on the isolating ring road, giving no clue as to the grandeur of the building. It is a four-bay brick box pierced with broad windows with Gothick arched tops. The glazing is exceptionally elegant with interlocking Gothick arches and diamond-shaped quarries. At either end of the nave are two restrained Tuscan porches in stone with fine columns and pediments.

At the east end is a later nineteenth-century apse and at the west end a square tower.

Sounds good, eh? The perfect Georgian provincial town church. But approach it (to do so you will need to dive into the least favoured part of Upper Hanley, where the back of the lumpen Potteries Shopping Centre meets the ring road) and you will be saddened. For this, perhaps the best building in Hanley, is in a seriously advanced state of disrepair, panes broken, slates fallen, the cupola that is shown topping the smart church tower in an engraving of 1840 long since gone and the clock face staring blindly out of the ruined tower. The churchyard has, in an all too familiar way, been gobbled up with road and the much-reduced site is surrounded by easily permeable hoardings that fail to reduce vandalism. Its future? It is to be converted to use as a restaurant . . .

St Peter's, Burslem, should be better. The square tower is earlier, mid-sixteenth century, and on to it has been grafted what was obviously another fine eighteenth-century prayer box. Externally it is ruinous, covered in a gloomy cement render with the round-topped windows barricaded against projectiles. At the east end is a shallow and beautiful elliptical apse with a Venetian window above the altar. It is not an easy church to get into, but a letter I poked under the door elicited a quick response on the telephone the next day from the warden. The interior has been fine. A gallery survives, as do pews and several reminders of the church's connections with the early pottery industry, particularly the Wedgwood and Wood families. It is in use; it has a congregation and a Sunday school.

But it is desperately down at heel. The graves in the churchyard are a Potteries hall of fame: Wedgwoods, Adams and many other lesser potters of the eighteenth and nineteenth centuries lie beneath elegantly inscribed slabs. Monumental masonry did not keep up with the fashions, though, and the

STOKE MINSTER
TRUBSHAWE & JOHNSON
1826–1830
COMMISSIONERS' GOTHIC

ST BARTHOLOMEW'S BLURTON · Rebuilt 1626 in Red Coursed Sandstone

angels who flap above John Adams, 'late of Birches Head in this Parish who died January the 28th 1752 aged 83', feel as if they were drawn in the years of his youth and not the product of the refined eighteenth century. His son's tomb, however, a distinguished and massive edifice erected in 1778, is quite of the new Georgian style with a finely reeded frieze and a squat but correct Doric order with accurately chamfered panel within, announcing his death in 1774. These august potters, the creators of Stoke, lie among the Coke cans, glue tops and Peperami wrappers, cast off by their descendants. It is nearly impossible to picture them, stiff in provincial finery, parading past the churchyard, Bell or Fountain Works to worship at their fine parish church.

Commissioners' Gothic churches are thicker on the ground and Stoke has some particularly good examples of this rather strange phenomenon. In 1818 the Church Commissioners realized that the quickly growing population of England was outgrowing its places of worship; this was particularly the case in the new suburbs of London and in the new industrial towns of the north. Equally concerning was the fact that it was leaving the established church in droves for the more lively and fundamentalist establishments of the Nonconformist churches, such as the Baptists and the Unitarians. In a move predating by some twenty years the Gothic Revival that the young Augustus Pugin would instigate, the style selected for these designs was a superficial Regency gothic, neither the icing-sugar Gothick of Strawberry Hill nor the thoroughgoing early English or Decorated Revival that was to come. The churches were, in plan, unchanged from their classical contemporaries but clothed in a superficially gothic outfit. This produced a pattern-book design of little historical precedent and of no local character but nevertheless one that was instantly recognizable. It was also cheap, sometimes excessively so. Stoke has bad examples as well as good: for example, Christchurch in the very recently conceived area of Cobridge has decoration so slight as to be apologetic.

While these worthy but austere buildings were being hurriedly erected along with their vicarages or rectories, the Nonconformist movement was in full swing. John Wesley, father of Methodism, was particularly fond of Stoke and visited often, preferring the honest and plain-spoken Stoke-ites to their more refined silk-weaving equivalents at nearby Congleton. (This is, of course, an anecdote found in a book about Stoke.) His preaching, however, bore great fruits and consequently houses in which to spread the good news were built, many and varied. Some were also very large. Perhaps the finest of all is the Bethesda Chapel in the middle of Hanley. What the Commissioners' gothic churches lack in bravura is made up for in buckets by this baroque temple. A colonnade in the Corinthian order supports a deep balcony, behind which is a pedimented first floor. Beneath the colonnade fine doorcases in giant scale lead the pilgrim to a dignified hall, from which he or she passes into a vast horseshoe-shaped hall with steeply raised seats in box pews and a gallery above. The windows that light the room once contained stained glass by Burne-Jones which recently came to light in the store rooms of the City Museum. Although currently in what might politely be called a

Burslem Methodist Church 1960s...

state of flux, the Bethesda is a completely good-news story. A favoured contender for victory in BBC1's *Restoration* series in 2003 (in which various much-loved buildings in dire need of rescue biffed it out to win a substantial prize that would save them from desolation), it has been the subject of much voluntary laborious but extensive restoration work and a recipient of English Heritage grant money, and will in due course re-open to the public in a semblance of its former glory. (See also page 23.)

A less happy story but no less exciting a building is the Burslem Methodist Sunday School. Immediately west of the main square in Burslem and less than quarter of a mile down the hill is a gaunt portico. Massive Doric columns support a heavy frieze on which is written 'BURSLEM METHODIST SUNDAY SCHOOL'. It was once so powerful an institution that its Sunday classes attracted 800 children, for many of whom it represented the sole source of education. Now it might as well say, 'My name is Ozymandias, King of Kings,/Look on my works ye mighty and despair', so powerful is the message of change and decay that it embodies. It has been the subject of countless efforts to raze its embarrassing remains to the ground by its owners, and at times by the local council; but listing by English Heritage in 1999 has for a time staved that off. And despite its tired paintwork and sprouting buddlejas it is as moving and profoundly romantic ruin as Stoke has to offer, a Riveaulx or Fountains of the industrial Midlands.

WESTPORT METHODIST SUNDAY SCHOOL 1836. A Huge EDUCATIONAL ESTABLISHMENT, for many their ONLY EDUCATION.

These 8 Massive DORIC COLUMNS support an ENTABLATURE. They are Survivors of a fire of 1983. * AT RISK! *

Throughout Stoke are other chapels and temples, but some of the best are those attached to the cemeteries of the city. The ornate and well-conceived chapel and lodge of the Hanley cemetery is just such a building. A sophisticated exercise in late nineteenth-century Gothic Revival, it marks the entry to the resting place of many of the town's potters and other citizens. Immediately outside its main gateway is a polished granite and sandstone monument to Charles Meakin (see page 144). The graveyard of Stoke itself is even more dramatic, sloping gently down from the heights of Penkhull, the original settlement of that town. In it the sharply defined strata of nineteenth-century society are harshly defined. The current one-crematorium-fits-all situation is far and away the best of the series of chapels – first and second class, C. of E., Roman Catholic and Nonconformist – that dot the city.

The cemeteries of Stoke are peopled with potters. Outside the north door of Christchurch, Fenton, a genuinely plain building snubbed, rightly, by Pevsner as 'the magnum opus of Charles Lynam of Stoke-magnum, however, only in size', lies Charles Meath Baker. The Meath Bakers, one-time potters of Fenton but later more agreeably squires of Hasfield Court in Gloucestershire, not only funded the civic buildings of the town in which their business had thrived but also built some of the best model housing in the entire city in the Queen Anne Revival style, all sunflowers, terracotta panels and rubbed brick pediments. Inside St Peter Ad Vincula Stoke sit monuments to the first two Josiahs Spode, as well as Josiah Wedgwood, while other Wedgwoods and Woods lie in faded state in Burslem.

Oddest of the city's churches is the Church of the Sacred Heart, Tunstall (although St Joseph, Burslem, in high-fired engineering brick to match the emancipated Catholic zeal within is a contender. Stoke has always had a large proportion of Roman Catholics among its churchgoers, a reflection of the influx of industrial workers from Ireland). The singular outbreak of shallow copper-green domes flash as a landmark from a distance, but it is even more extraordinary at close confines. Pevsner enigmatically describes it as 'Large and eager to impress', and it certainly is both. Despite its being rich in the Victorian spirit of historicism, it was built between 1925 and 1930 and designed by both J.S. Brockesby and the incumbent, Fr P.J. Ryan. Its west front, much compromised by its situation among the terraces, is a wild and unguarded fantasy reminiscent of the great westworks of the Romanesque cathedrals of northern Europe, all towers and turrets and conical roofs, while the slightly less vocal north and south elevations are in a fairly robust neo-Norman with some Perp thrown in for fun. All this be-buttressed and bound-about work is in a dark-brown brick that seems sooty black, all the more to throw into relief the shocking green domes clustered like Shiva's many bosoms on the roof. It is a wonderfully odd building.

Behind is a mean alley of cobbles, like those still relatively common in Stoke but with a difference. The retaining wall of the churchyard is a remarkable bit of Stoke vernacular, as it is built of a strange conglomerate of cement, sand and disused kiln furniture. On closer inspection its surface reveals thousands of buff-coloured fireclay components jumbled together and preserved like industrial fossils in industrial marble.

The population of admirably economical and self-effacing Jews built a modest box-like synagogue in Hanley, now abandoned by its tiny congregation, who no meet in a still less effusive establishment at the gate of Newcastle hospital. The community's leader mourns the near-disappearance of a Jewish population once more than 400. with a reticence missing among the mosques that are currently under construction. Perhaps the growing Muslim population could use some of the great and unused churches as mosques (this has worked well at Hagia Sophia in Istanbul, after all) – surely a better use for a temple of Nonconformism or even a parish church than as a carpet warehouse? If buildings are to survive, they need a use and there seem to be missed opportunities here. Preservation for its own sake is fine as a temporary measure, but a genuine match between building and use is the only long-term solution.

METHODIST CHURCH · OLD TOWN Rd
HANLEY 1860
LATER (1926) SPIRITUALIST CHURCH
LATER © 2005
RESTAURANT
∴
SAVED...

(16) TOWER OF St JOHN the BAPTIST . BURSLEM

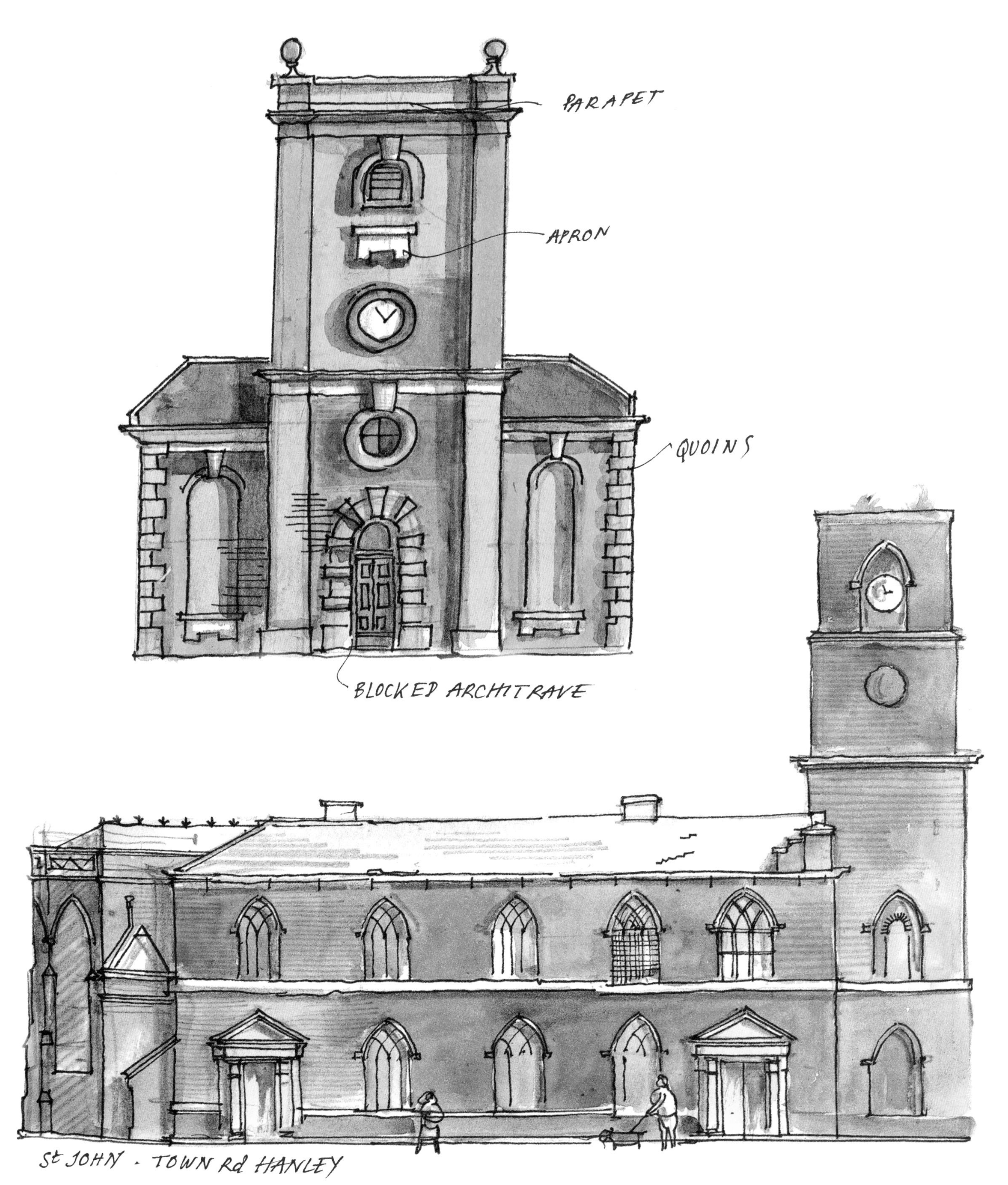
PARAPET
APRON
QUOINS
BLOCKED ARCHITRAVE
St JOHN - TOWN Rd HANLEY

CEMETERY CHAPELS
HANLEY · 1860
ON EITHER side of
steepled Arch
ARE TWO CHAPELS,
one C of E (L·H·S)
and one for
NON-CONFORMISTS
CREMATORIUM CHAPEL at CARMOUNTSIDE

STABLES for the VICARAGE
CHRISTSCHURCH
COBRIDGE.
COMMISSIONERS' GOTHIC
at its most MEAGRE
As with all pre-PUGIN
C19 Gothic building
this is basically a
classical BUILDING
in GOTHIC TRIM
ST MARK'S SHELTON –
a more GENEROUS
com' GOTHIC. 1831.
J. OATES of HALIFAX

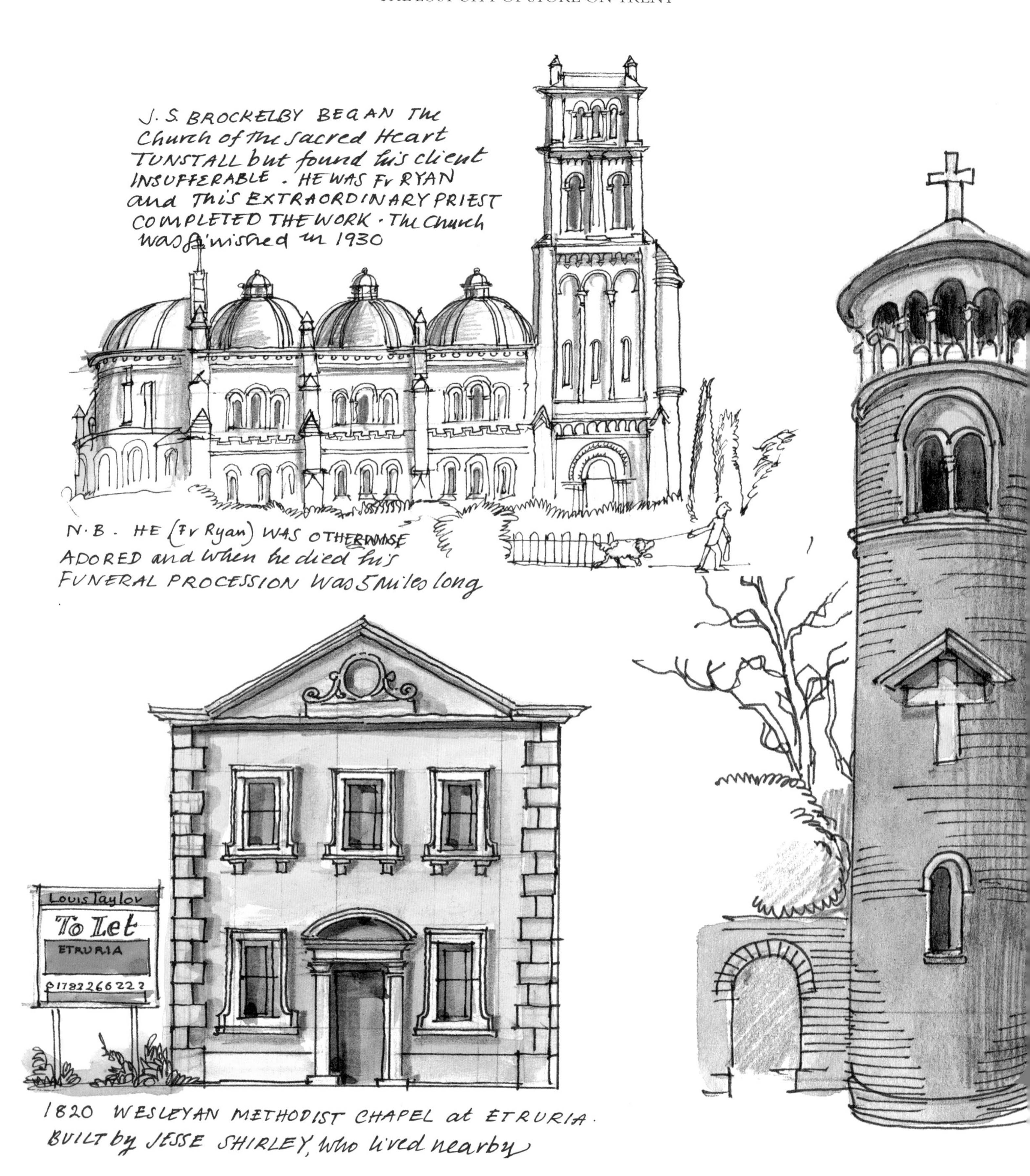

1820 WESLEYAN METHODIST CHAPEL at ETRURIA. BUILT by JESSE SHIRLEY, who lived nearby

ST JOSEPH'S ROMAN CATHOLIC CHURCH
BURSLEM 1925-27 J.S. BROCKESBY
A BIZARRE & WONDERFULLY IDIOSYNCRATIC CHURCH.

BETHEL CHAPEL ONE of the two Great NON-CONFORMIST CATHEDRALS of the CITY

BURSLEM NATIONAL SCHOOL c 1800

BETHESDA
METHODIST CHURCH
LORD'S DAY
DIVINE WORSHIP 10·45
MINISTER
REV. Dr O. BECKERLEGGE
128 REGENT Rd MA
HANLEY
TELE. STOKE ON TRENT 2418
CHAPEL KEEPER Mr GIBSON
33 RE
The BIRTHPLACE of The NEW CONNEXION
THE GREAT SUCCESS THAT IS The NEARLY RESTORED BETHESDA CHAPEL
1819 Then more 1859 & 1887 on the DEED of The ORIGINAL TRUST
were the POTTERS : JOB & GEORGE RIDGWAY RICHARD HIX & JOB MEIGH

STOKE RIGHT NOW

Last week I drove from Oxford to Stoke with a friend, a friend who had never been north of Watford Gap and whose life has all been spent in London and the south. We drove along the M6 Toll, a road still so empty that when on it you feel as if you are driving in France, and then rejoined the M6 proper. The last bit of Staffordshire through which that motorway passes is beautiful country, gently rolling with neat plantations sitting comfortably on the sides of modest hills. Just before exit fifteen a glance to the right is rewarded with the site of Barlaston Hall, the first sign of Stoke.

The interchange, embanked and thickly planted with birch and larch, makes a tunnel of anywhere-in-Britain before the A500 sweeps majestically into the Trent valley. Dramatically, and sadly not uncharacteristically, as we drove along it a pall of cloud and rain hovered over the city and my friend gasped. For even now, after fifty years of cleaning up and tidying away, the industrial nature of the view is striking. Chimneys still smoke and dominate the skyline and tower blocks do not. A newcomer can be bowled over by the otherness of Stoke, it being so profoundly unlike the sophisticated, glossy south.

Yet there is nothing genuinely shocking about Stoke. It looks and feels like a post-industrial city, but quite a small one. It does not have the high-energy buzz of Manchester, Glasgow or Leeds, nor the utter desolation of Billingham or the reconstructed commercial engine of Birmingham. Its smaller size and very decidedly provincial nature characterize it completely. It is definitively not a regional capital – not a Norwich. That city, not so different in population, serves an area the size of Holland as capital. There is no comparable urban centre southwards before London, north before Lincoln or Hull, west before Birmingham or east before Amsterdam, and so it takes on some of the metropolitan nature of those distant neighbours in terms of cultural, financial, legal and social function. In contrast Stoke does, of course, have law courts, theatres and banks, but these are secondary to those in nearby Manchester and Birmingham, and it is to these two great cities that the fanatical shopper travels at Christmas or for the January sales.

Retail is one of the great engines of Britain. Some of our largest companies are retailers – the grocers, the store groups and the smaller chains of fashion shops and coffee shops. Stoke is not uppermost on their screens. It does not have a Waitrose or a John Lewis, signals of a lucrative retail area. Its shopping centre has no Pret A Manger, Café Nero, Space NK, Jigsaw or Monsoon, let alone the glossier fashion brands. This is not, of course, to say that people do not shop in the city; Hanley, which is the commercial centre of the place, is busy, particularly on a Wednesday, market day, when the central precinct is full of plant stalls, dog beds and pillows, now the staple goods of markets the world over. But Stoke is not a focus for sophisticated retail. This is not Stoke bashing. Failure to conform to high-street orthodoxy might even seem to be a good thing to some. But it does present a problem. For it is to retail that councils and developers automatically turn when seeking to regenerate a city centre, and this is what is currently being undertaken in Stoke at the moment.

Urban regeneration works. It has worked in Gateshead and Gloucester, Bristol and Birmingham, and Manchester. The equation of construction + clearance + jobs + influx of investment = economic regeneration seems to work. Particularly successful have been schemes where canal, river or port have been the focus of these projects, as at Castlefield in Manchester, where flats and office space, some newly built and others cleverly converted from warehouses and factories, are woven between the canals, viaducts and railway bridges of the nineteenth-century heyday of that city; or the Gloucester Docks, where the distinguished nineteenth-century quayside warehouses have become NHS and council offices and thus dodged the wrecker's concrete ball. Stoke seems to be perfectly suited to this treatment. After all, two canals wind through the city, providing plenty of opportunity for just this kind of development. The factories that were built all along these eighteenth- and nineteenth-century thoroughfares would seem to lend themselves to just the kind of sensitive conversion that has worked so well in Manchester or Birmingham – or would do if the majority of them had not already been smashed down to provide developers with a blank canvas. (A developer's blank canvas is a tricky concept of course, blank canvases traditionally being in need of artistic intervention.)

Industrial areas are not the sole focus for regeneration: other industrial towns have also taken the base material of terraced housing and, through a clever rethinking of this housing type, updated and transformed these areas. Companies like Urban Splash have developed a language within which to work, removing parts of each terrace, or on occasion whole terraces, to introduce much needed green space (these were, of course, once called parks and are now correctly termed 'public realm') and to create flats and houses that people actually want.

Stoke City Council is much abused, often quite justly. It has overseen much vacuous and flimsy reconstruction, misguided development and unfocused planning. Those wanting an example of the vapid and hopeless kind of building erected under their control need look no further than Potteries Way. Prominently situated Stoke's worst crashingly unfunny architectural bad joke is particularly visible, commanding one of the road's best-used interchanges. It seems to be made of paper and garishly coloured matchsticks. Each elevation sits under an insulting quasi-pediment and as if in comment on the banal design its tenants have plastered the windows with posters and flimsy plastic signage that, despite their ephemeral nature, seem to dominate the slight structure.

Under the council's less than watchful eye a lot of what has been best about Stoke has been demolished and little of what remains has really been maintained. A bone-headed reluctance to perceive the area's internationally famous industrial past as anything more than an embarrassment and a silly desire to make the place a pallid imitation of urban models that are anyway of limited appeal have done little to improve this situation. But perhaps City Hall has had a rather tricky job. Perhaps the frayed mesh of post-industrial survivors, run-down terraces and desperate poor-quality retail and leisure parks is in fact really intractable, its undisciplined plan and the five/six towns with their town halls and institutes a genuine puzzle. Perhaps it is difficult to imagine the economic (and thus political) stranglehold in which the Big Potters held the city. Their interests were paramount and to cross or refuse them was impossible; and not surprisingly they were disliked. However, the council's revenge on the pottery industry, albeit wreaked not on the companies but on their discarded architectural remnants, has been harsh.

The current phase of reconstruction is one of a long line of similar efforts. First there was slum clearance before and after the last war. The 1960s saw a plan drawn up for a new-technology-led regeneration of the city. The 1970s was a period in which the marl pits and coal mines with their heaps of shraff or waste – of old moulds and broken pottery – were filled or flattened, literally one pushed into the other before being remodelled into a sort of tree-and-scrub-covered non-landscape. Writing in 1978, Bill Morland in *Portrait of the Potteries* describes the process with breathless enthusiasm for the spirit of the age:

The most obvious change is in the landscape. Marl holes are now fields and ornamental lakes, pit heaps have vanished, there is no longer a pall of smoke over the valleys; a brave new face is beginning to smile through the moonscapes of the past . . . now we have a forest park. A combination of the hugeness of a forest with the landscapability of a park. Instead of gravel paths we have cinder tracks, no more are there borders of wallflowers, the old walls themselves flower with lichen and fern . . . at the same time the Westport Lake park was completed and . . . a nautical Prime Minister came to open its forty-nine acres of sailing facilities and picnic areas.

Perhaps Shakespeare intended Miranda's marvelling in *The Tempest* at a 'brave new world/That has such people in it' to include a note of irony, but I think not. There is always a touching faith in the new and that a rejection of the past will be intrinsically good, leading inexorably to a better world.

In the post-war clear-up of Britain the brave-new-world-ish approach to planning was dominant among those who were reconstructing the country. Dramatic and to contemporary eyes unthinkably destructive plans were drawn up to wipe away the tired old city centres, their situation often aggravated by wartime bomb damage. Just such a plan survives for Norwich, with futuristic artistic renderings of a new civic centre, wide spacious boulevards, clean modern lines and an utter clearance of a medieval street plan. Somehow common sense, usually the produce of a lack of available funds, prevented this Scandinavian utopia from becoming reality. In the 1970s, however, St Ebbe's, the warren of medieval streets and courts that made up a significant part of central Oxford, was swept away to the wails of aesthetic laments from north Oxford to be replaced, in part, by a Brutalist shopping centre, built in a style that is now commonly acknowledged by developer and tweedy art historian alike to be an unparalleled disaster; indeed it is shortly to be removed.

The utopian project for greening Stoke was followed by the Garden Festival of 1986. The great sheds of Shelton Bar iron works (so large were these works, established by the Earls Granville in the early nineteenth century, that they coloured the night-time skies red) and the wasteland that was Wedgwood's Etruria were remodelled, making Etruria Hall the centre of a huge flower show with model gardens, cascades and rockeries – something that had been successful three years previously in Gateshead. The area was subsequently turned into a new eyesore to replace the old industrial ones: the worst sort of retail 'park' with supermarkets and a multiplex cinema, all placed within a formless plan designed for car access only and so more road than building. This has proved to be the perfect place for opportunistic boys who spend the evenings comparing customized vehicles and then racing them about the empty car parks before being moved along by the police, although this boy racing is perfectly benign and most of the time the cars are parked window to open window, providing opportunity for conversation. The whole area is an example of the now-discredited planning policy of zoning, in which each building use – residential, commercial, retail and industrial – was kept apart. This was in itself a reaction to the hugger-mugger unplanned proximity of slum to factory in the nineteenth century.

Now there is more planning, more masterplans and more bodies to administer them, although with a new approach.

There is at last a realization that it is the industrial past and, more excitingly, the industrial present of the Potteries that is their only hope and that building on this tradition – the extraordinary heritage of Wegdwood and Minton, Mason's and Spode, Adams and Wood and Ridgway and New Hall and Aynsley and the dozens of companies that have started, faltered, stopped or started again – is the way to rebuild Stoke as something real and outstanding. This is far from easy. In answer to an enquiry about a brownfield residential site in Hanley a property developer said : 'It will happen but it's got to happen to a lot of other places first before that becomes viable.' Stoke has a low-value property sector but a high-value pottery industry and with that an increasingly significant tourism industry. Every year thousands of Japanese come to see the Wedgwood Visitor Centre and first-rate museum. Perhaps they would like to see the Spode museum as well. Home-bred tourists from all over the country come to look around factories that make a recognizable product – something that has become increasingly difficult.

There have been few examples yet of really good development in the city. First-rate refurbishment of good terraced housing in Hanley, new pavements and retaining walls, reinstatement of porches and other improvements have provided optimistic proof of a really credible alternative to blanket demolition of terraces that are built to a standard to which no new housing project could aspire, the hackneyed orthodoxy of newer energy-efficient housing being shot to pieces when the embodied carbon that is tied up in existing structures is taken into the equation.

The new mantras of preservation and conservation are not yet being chanted quite loudly enough in the corridors of Stoke's City Hall, but they are creeping in and will be heard more clearly. The critical issue is whether the great factories, churches and chapels, pubs and the terraces of neat Victorian housing, the pottery owners and managers' houses and the municipal palaces of one of the great cities of the first Industrial Revolution in the world can wait. Will they stay upright (if tatty) while Stoke catches up with its bigger neighbours, Birmingham and Manchester? Or will they fall foul of an understandable near-desperation among those who are genuinely trying to regenerate the place and be flattened to create the 'blank canvas' seen as so desirable to a previous generation of planners?

I really hope they make it. I hope that they stumble on and that when the time is right for the city of Stoke to be rebuilt, when there are people really crying out for new homes (of all sizes), which means when there are thousands of job vacancies needing to filled, there will still be some fragments of that place's history left to provide the cultural backbone of a new Stoke.

EPILOGUE AT EASTWOOD

I have been a potter 51 years, first as a moulder; and have through every department; am now the overlooker or manager of the works. It is my duty to hire and discharge all the hands. We employ now, being low, 348 persons, that is 125 males 69 females, adults; 42 males, 71 female, under 21; 23 boys, 18 girls, under 13.

The premises stand upon about three acres, more or less: and consist of 60 rooms; seven ovens, and five offices, well drained and lighted by candles; there is no engine of any kind except jiggers. The people come at six in the summer, and seven in the winter, and leave at six; there is sometimes over-work when orders come in; and they work 'till nine. The plate-makes, saucer-makers, and bowlers take on their boys with the consent of the overlooker, and pay them by the day. All paid by the master, are paid in hard cash. We sometimes for the people advance sums of money, and let them work it out; we sometimes do that with the men, and let the boys work it out, or girls, but we have no such thing as written contracts with parents for the employment of children. All advances are made for the benefit of the people, and are considered favours. We should not advance money to a drunken character.

We consider the dipping as the most unhealthy process in the department, that indeed is the only one; the scouring is bad, but the women do not continue long in it; they get married and leave. I think potters' children are tolerably healthy; they look white, but that is from the clay, which is not pernicious. We have no boys as painters in the works, the painting is done here by men and women.

I do not know that I have any other information to give.

A potter in Hanley, 1850

But I have . . .

1851 was the year of the Great Exhibition, that swollen, bulging glass showcase of the second wind of Britain's Industrial Revolution. The same year saw the establishment of the partnership of two potter brothers, James and George Meakin. So well did the enterprise go that in 1859 the business moved to new premises in Hanley called the Eagle Works. Their brother Charles had meanwhile established the Eastwood Works close by on Lichfield Street. In 1887 the three joined together and formed J. and G. Meakin; 'their aim', says that company's history, 'was to sell reliable, serviceable and good looking pottery to the peoples of the Americas, the Dominions, and the Colonies and their factory in Hanley was planned accordingly'. George had spent some time in the States, living in Boston, and had built up the connections necessary to establishing a booming transatlantic business. They built Eastwood works in 1880.

By 1954 the founders' grandchildren were running the business in such a way that it was described as 'among the most modern and well planned of factories, capable of producing anything most likely to be demanded of it'. It was producing one million pieces every week.

And they were a strange selection. This coffee pot was made in 1965. It is marked 'Studio J and G Meakin' and is a jolly odd piece. The attenuated spout curves gracefully from one side, while on the opposite face a clumsy, if ergonomically comfortable, handle sticks baldly out. The decoration is printed on to the piece in imitation of spongeware, although in a design with quite different inspiration: it was called Aztec. Neither the shape nor the decorative devices would have been particularly familiar to the Amerindian natives busily employed at their human sacrifice on the steps of those great Mexican temples; indeed it is hard to see exactly from where they are derived. The pot is not a piece of great beauty and must wait several more decades before it can be anything other than an acquired taste. Other designs were more traditional and olde English in feeling, or faintly Scandinavian.

In fact those one million pieces were symptomatic of the problem that within fifty years would reduce the business of Stoke-on-Trent to a very different scale, where the entire industry might only turn out a million pieces per week. The pottery that came through the loading bays of the Eagle and Eastwood Works was rather ordinary and the sort of thing that fills the short white china shelves of the shops of Oxfam, Cancer Research UK and the rest. It was the boring sub-Willow-pattern or the brown floral border or the lifeless flock of mallard that you ignore in the junk shop and the public were becoming bored.

J. and G. Meakin continued until the year 2000, when it was sold to Johnson Brothers, part of the Wedgwood group, who – in a familiar tale – promptly shut it down and in 2004 the company was no more. The Eastwood site had already been sold to Emma Bridgewater in 1994.

Emma Bridgewater set up her eponymous business in 1985, sensing an emerging market for more informal earthenware for a more sophisticated customer. This was not a cynical marketing exercise, as she was her own model customer. She had found it impossible to find the ideal cup and saucer as birthday present for her mother and so decided to produce them herself. I am Emma's husband and so tread warily here to avoid hagiographic pitfalls . . .

By 1994 the business had developed to the extent that its then factory in Longbridge Hayes in Stoke was bursting at the seams and the thirty employees could not swing a jug. While the company was looking for another factory, Eastwood came into focus. The 3-acre site was virtually empty. The factory shop was conveniently central enough for Wedgwood to maintain stock and staff there, principally of the now foreign-made Johnson Brothers products, which were at the lowest end of their market. In the casting shop were two huge automatic casting benches. These machines were able to produce 5,000 cups each a day, but they were cups that nobody wanted and at a price that still could not compete with the low-wage economies of the palm-fringed China Seas. There were also fettling and sponging machines, capable of finishing countless thousands of pieces every week but not to fulfil a need.

Emma and I walked through the factory. The Lichfield Street rooms were (indeed still are) 250 feet long – longer by twice than the Hall of Mirrors at Versailles. The roof was supported with vast trusses, the members of which measure 3 feet by 18 inches, and the façade, at thirty bays, was, and remains, as long as that of Chatsworth or Castle Howard. Through the first-floor windows of the original J. and G. Meakin decorating shop we looked across the dun-brown Cauldon canal, into which swallows were diving for water, to the ruins of the Imperial Works, once part of the extensive home of Johnson Brothers. Its curving façade, built to exactly the same specifications as that of Eastwood, elegantly traced the curve of the canal but was a façade only, the building behind already pulverized. That curve led the eye on to the semi-transparent skeleton-ruin of the Hanley Works, with its jaunty pale-blue paintwork flaking into the empty courtyards, which had recently been another of Johnson's manufactories. Beyond, the terraces of southern Hanley led to Fenton and to the demolished quarter of Joiners Square. Behind the factory, heading up to the city centre, were terraces of blackened brick artisan houses, their back roofs sloping down to smaller and smaller spans of kitchen and privy and then to the alley that separated them from the back of the next street.

Within the factory yards the stuff of the building was so homogenous and so unaltered that there were places where we could look through 360 degrees and see only the nineteenth century. This factory, which was so utterly typical of dozens of similar ones that recently dominated Stoke-on-Trent, was fast becoming remarkable. We bought the building, but what we did not know, when we moved the business to it, was that ten years later it would have turned from uncommon into a rarity. The industry was slipping away then, but the most significant losses have taken place in the last fifteen years and are going on now as I write in 2010.

How different is Eastwood today from the factory described at the beginning of this chapter! In the buildings work 150 people: 2 men mixing clay in the slip house, 15 casters, 2 bowl makers, 1 plate maker, 20 spongers and fettlers, 4 furnace men and 4 placers, 2 backstampers and 2 polishers, 25 spongeware decorators and 10 litho decorators, 8 selectors, 20 warehouse men, 2 builders, a joiner, a decorator and an electrician. We have an office with 10 more people and 4 in the design studio. In the factory shop, decorating studio and café (an area unthought of in 1859) there are another dozen. The factory is like a small village, a working community with marriages, births and deaths, romances and gossip, theft and injury, scandal and excitement.

These are to all intents the same jobs described by the potter of 1850 and with the exception of the electric light and gas and electric kilns the scene would be completely familiar to him. Do his great-great-grandchildren work here? I asked the decorators how many had parents and grandparents who had worked in the industry. Most had worked 'on a potbank', and most assumed that the tradition went back further, perhaps for eight generations. This is a snapshot in 2010, but perhaps it's the last one of its kind; if there are only 6,000 ceramics workers in the business, there are so few sets of grandparents left. It is like the breezy smiles on white flannelled and boatered undergraduates in a sepia photograph of 1913. If the industry continues to shrink, this extraordinary continuity will stop dead and as in the mining towns of Yorkshire or the cotton towns of Lancashire that thread to the past will snap. And that will change for ever the character of a city from one whose very existence revolves around pottery to one that once made it. Does that matter?

While Eastwood is still working, Old Eastwood House, which looked over the land on which the factory is built, is gone, as are its gardens with the ilex grove and the summerhouse and the donkey with the leather shoes pulling the mower. No more leopard-spotted specimens are exotically reclining in the half-sunken mossy orchid house cut into the rock with the boiler smelling coaly behind the bay tree. The Portuguese laurels have grown and been felled. All the garden plans came off and then to nothing. The cedar

of Lebanon, focus of several quite dull explanations to children at garden parties on whom the whole idea of the wisdom of Solomon was wasted and who only waited impatiently for the cakes and buns in their Sunday stiffness has been felled and sold as firewood.

Daisy Piece, Haines Meadow and Shaw Croft, the field names marked on the 1860 map of the estate, are enclosures gone for ever, along with Upper and Lower Pith, Lower Field and Shaw Croft. The lower half of Shaws Croft became the flint mill that Charles Meakin made into his factory; the upper half became housing. In 2005 the council started the piecemeal demolition of these terraces, places where the casters and fettlers at Eastwood had lived and died, rolled home drunk or quietly, and in the crowded little houses initiated new generations of potters. Some stuck it out. But the last owners, still passing the ghosts of their neighbours on their way to the shops or into town, had to give in and the last houses were stoved in, along with a banner announcing 'Welcome to Beirut'.

The demolition workers departed, leaving the blocks between the roads quite flat and enclosed by low bunds of earth to stop playful young motorcyclists from turning them into dirt tracks. The ground settled and although it was quite biblical in its stoniness, an unholy mix of cinder, brick fragments and old asbestos, it came to life. The next spring it began to green. The normal local-authority urge to strim and trim was stymied by the bunds and the plants grew. By July each plot was spotted with colour: poppies, cornflowers, heartsease and even corncockle had burst their seed bank and 150 years after the last crop of wheat was cut there in the 1870s Shaw Croft was ablaze. The seeds had lain dormant, waiting for the ground to be turned again. Along with the arable weeds are other leftovers – snapdragons and calendula and anchusa – surviving in the same way, but this time from the gardens of the pottery workers.

And there are still men in white overalls discussing the cricket and the football as inside the works they make mugs and jugs and bowls. There are still fifty ladies leaving in time to collect the children from school; still kilns to load and unload, clay to scrape with an ash-handled shovel. This is Stoke today.

LIST OF POTTERIES

A list of long-established potters working in 1954, indicating date of establishment and whether currently operating in 2010.

NAME OF BUSINESS	LOCATION	DATE ESTABLISHED	CURRENT STATUS
William Adams and Sons	Tunstall	1657	defunct
Amison and Co.	Longton	1875	defunct
George Ashworth	Hanley	1807	defunct
John Aynsley and Sons	Longton	1775	active
Barrats	Burslem	1828	defunct
Beswick	Longton	1897	defunct
Biltons	Stoke	1912	active
Bluejohn pottery	Hanley	1886	defunct
Booth and Colclough	Stoke	1757	defunct
Bourne	Fenton	1809	defunct
Brain	Fenton	1850	defunct
Thos Brian	Longton	1880	defunct
Bridgwood	Longton	1820	defunct
British Anchor	Longton	1884	defunct
Broadhurst	Fenton	1847	defunct
Burgess and Leigh	Burslem	1851	active
Cauldon	Stoke	1774	defunct
Chapmans	Longton	1916	defunct
Coalport China	Stoke	1750	defunct [*but remains as a brand name as part of Wedgwood*]
Collingwood	Longton	1796	defunct
Coopers	Hanley	1894	defunct
Copeland	Stoke	1770	defunct [*but Spode as a brand remains as a division of Portmeirion*]
Cotton	Hanley	1885	defunct
Crown Staffordshire	Fenton	1801	defunct
Dennis	Fenton	1889	defunct
Doulton	Burslem	1815	defunct
Dudson	Tunstall	1800	active
Ford and sons	Burslem	1865	defunct
Furnivalls	Cobridge	1913	defunct
Gladstone	Longton	1870	Museum
Grindley	Longton	1850	defunct
Hammersley	Longton	1850	defunct

NAME OF BUSINESS	LOCATION	DATE ESTABLISHED	CURRENT STATUS
Keele Pottery	Tunstall	1917	defunct
James Kent	Longton	1686	defunct
Kirkhams	Stoke	1859	defunct
Lancaster and Sandland	Hanley	1884	defunct
Lawrence	Longton	1885	defunct
Linguard	Tunstall	1867	defunct
Maddock	Burslem	1820	defunct
Meakin , Alfred	Tunstall	1873	defunct
Meakin J. and G.	Hanley	1851	defunct
Minton	Stoke	1790	defunct [*surviving in part as a sub-brand of Doulton, itself a part of Wedgwood*]
Moorcroft	Burslem	1913	active
Myott	Hanley	1880	defunct
New Chelsea China	Hanley	1899	defunct
New Hall	Hanley	1900 [*and earlier*]	defunct
Palissy	Longton	1855	defunct
Paragon	Hanley	1897	defunct
Plant	Longton	1884	defunct
Radford	Fenton	1883	defunct
Richardson	Cobridge	1915	defunct
Rosina	Longton	1875	defunct
Roslynn	Longton	1911	defunct
Royal Staffordshire China	Burslem	1845	active
Sadler	Burslem	1882	defunct
Sampson	Longton	1886	defunct
Shelley	Longton	1867	defunct
Simpson	Cobridge	1706	defunct
Sylvan	Hanley	1886	defunct
Tams	Longton	1774	defunct
Wedgwood	Burslem	1759	active
Wild	Longton	1894	defunct
Wood, Arthur	Longport	1884	defunct
Wood and Sons	Burslem	1750	defunct

N.B. This is part of a much longer list made up as much by companies founded after 1918. Names like Wetherby, Wade Heath or Midwinter are typical of well-known names as yet unfounded at that date; others are without a foundation date. Nevertheless the point is clear. Fifty years ago hundreds of companies made pottery in Stoke; now almost all are gone.

Of today's main surviving companies, which include Wedgwood, Portmeirion/Spode, Dudson, Steelite, Churchill, Wade, Emma Bridgewater, Caverswall, Burgess and Leigh, Duchess, Leedsware, Hudson and Middleton and Aynsley, about ten are entirely new, i.e. post-1958.

SOME INTERESTING PLACES TO VISIT

Wedgwood Visitor Centre
Barlaston
Stoke-on-Trent
ST12 9ER
Tel. 01782 371902
wedgwoodvisitorcentre.com

The Potteries Museum & Art Gallery
Bethesda Street, Hanley
Stoke-on-Trent
Tel. 01782 232323
stoke.gov.uk/museum

The Dudson Museum
Hope Street
Hanley
Stoke-on-Trent
ST1 5DD
Tel. 01782 285286
dudson.com

Gladstone Pottery Museum
Uttoxeter Road
Langton
ST3 1PQ
Tel. 01782 237777
stoke.gov.uk/museum

Etruria Industrial Museum
Lower Bedford Street
Stoke-on-Trent
ST4 7AF
Tel. 01782 233144
stoke.gov.uk/museum

Moorcroft
Sandbach Road
Burslem
ST6 2DQ
Tel. 01782 820515
moorcoft.com

Burgess and Leigh
Middleport
Burslem
ST6 3PE
Tel. 01782 577866
burleigh.co.uk

Emma Bridgewater
Eastwood Works
Lichfield Street
Te. 0844 243 9255
emmabridgewater.co.uk

N.B. Stoke has potters' holidays, the wakes weeks of the nineteenth century, so factories are shut for a week at Easter, two weeks in June and one at the end of August. Call to check before visiting. I have not included factory shops in this list, but there are plenty.

Other places to visit if you stay the night:

Chatsworth
Bakewell
Derbyshire
DE45 1PP
Tel. 01246 565300

Quarry Bank Mill
Styal
Wilmslow
SK9 4LA
Tel. 01625 415199

Arkwright's Mill
Cromford
Matlock
Derbyshire
DE4 3RQ
Tel. 01629 823256

Salts Mill
Victoria Road
Shipley
Saltaire
West Yorkshire
BD18 3LF
Tel. 01274 531163

National Trust
Little Moreton Hall
Congleton
Cheshire
CW12 4SD
Tel. 01260 272018

Sudbury Hall Museum of Childhood
Sudbury
Ashbourne
Derbyshire
DE6 5HT
Tel. 01283585305

INDEX

LOVE · STOKE
E · STOKE · LOV